THE Devil's Playground

STEVE RUSSO

HARVEST HOUSE PUBLISHERS
Eugene, Oregon 97402

THE DEVIL'S PLAYGROUND

Copyright © 1994 by Harvest House Publishers
Eugene, Oregon 97402

Library of Congress Cataloging-in-Publication Data

Russo, Steve, 1953-
    The devil's playground : playing with fire can get you burned /
Steve Russo.
        p. cm.
    ISBN 1-56507-043-7
    1. Devil—Controversial literature.   2. Satanism—Controversial
literature.   3. New Age movement—Controversial literature.
4. Occultism—Religious aspects—Christianity.   5. Teenagers—
Religious life.   I. Title.
BT981.R88   1994
235'.4—dc20   93-33945
                                                                CIP

Printed in the United States of America.

*Dedicated to the many students who have experienced
the deception of the darkness
and through Jesus were ultimately able
to stand up to the devil*

Contents

PART ONE

What You're Up Against

1

Satan's Targets

Dan and his buddies from school spent many late nights tapped into an obscure world of computer bulletin boards, conversing with other computer users by modem. They were especially hooked on two of the networks: "South of Heaven" and "The Infernal Flame." In his room, above his computer terminal, Dan painted a white pentagram on a stereo speaker. He also started using the names "Sid" and "Master Lucifer" on computer records.

Dan and his friends gradually began experimenting with some satanic rituals. They performed eerie ceremonies at midnight, burning pieces of their hair and fingernails. Dan started flunking out of school and, according to his teachers, developed an attention disorder.

▼ ▼ ▼

Fourteen-year-old Karen had an unreasonable fear of fire and cone-shaped objects. She also struggled with night terrors of hideous creatures in robes and braided hair sitting on the edge of her bed. But the worst thing of all was trying to ignore the voices in her head. They just kept bugging her with crazy and bizarre thoughts.

▼ ▼ ▼

Tony was 15 when his friends gave him a copy of Anton LaVey's *Satanic Bible*, a book which spells out the doctrine of Satanism. Tony's mind was so affected by the drugs he was taking that as he read the book, it began to sink in. Up to this point, he had been insecure and searching for something outside himself that would make him feel different. He liked the new attitude that the *Satanic Bible* gave him. Now he felt above people he used to be afraid to talk to. After all, he was a Satanist. The others only believed in God.

▼ ▼ ▼

When Lisa was in junior high she got kicked out of the house by her adoptive parents. She lived on the streets for about a year, then decided to go to the West Coast and try to start a new life.

In Hollywood she met some people who invited her to a birthday party where she was introduced to 22-year-old Bryan. That night Lisa learned he was possessed by some sort of spirit that claimed to be an old merchant seaman from five centuries ago.

This spirit suddenly spoke directly to Lisa in a voice she thought sounded familiar—the voice of her father from a previous lifetime. Lisa believed that 500 years ago, at the age of 11, she had been brutally raped and murdered while her father was on one of his many voyages to a far-off land. She and her father never had a chance to say good-bye. So it was a great surprise for her to talk with him once again after all these years. And now whenever she wants to speak to her "daddy," she just calls Bryan who enters a trance so she can talk to him.

Today, at the age of 16, Lisa is a Wiccan witch in training. After searching for truth and spiritual meaning in her life for a long time, she thinks she may have finally found it.

▼ ▼ ▼

Bob committed his life to Christ at an early age and was involved in his church youth group—going every Sunday morning and Wednesday night, plus summer and winter camps.

But Bob was bored. He was bored with school, church, and life in general. So he started playing Dungeons and Dragons, but he quickly became bored with the standard game and came up with his own version. Then he began to develop a hunger for evil and violence, yet he couldn't seem to get enough from television, movies, or the videos he rented. He hungered for more—the more violent, the better. The hunger was so great that he started reading books about the undead just because he could make the pictures so much more violent and colorful in his mind using his imagination.

His cousin invited him to a party where he smoked a joint for the first time. He was hooked. Drugs took away the boredom. He really got into the party scene and started going every week. Bob gradually progressed from marijuana to cocaine and eventually he took LSD. Amazingly, during this whole time, his parents had no clue about what he was doing.

Then Bob was invited to a "special party" by an older college guy who had been hanging around the parties. Not knowing for sure what this "special party" was, Bob hesitated at first, but he finally agreed to go.

Bob's ride picked him up that next weekend and took him outside the city limits to a large house in the middle of an orchard. The owner ushered them down to the basement where there were another 18 to 20 people. Every kind of liquor and drug imaginable was there. The host encouraged Bob to help himself to whatever he wanted—it was all free. So Bob got stoned and drunk with everybody else. Then people began getting undressed and pairing off for sex in a huge orgy. When that was over, everyone was invited to a side room of the basement.

There was a red goat's head painted on the wall and a pentagram in the middle of the floor. They all sat on the floor and began to chant strange-sounding songs. In a short time a blue-white spirit appeared in the center of the pentagram. Then the leaders of this satanic coven asked this spirit to harm a man in town who was bothering them. They chanted some more and sent the spirit on its way.

Three days later this man had a near-fatal accident. Bob was amazed by the instantaneous results of the satanic chant—and he was hooked. He finally found the power that he had been searching for. He had never seen anything like this—not even in the church.

So Bob began making a weekly journey to this isolated house for the "special party." The pattern was always the same: drugs, sex, and then the special ceremony in the side room of the basement. This continued for several months, and Bob began to sense the presence of a new power. He now had the ability to change things in his life for the first time. But it scared him.

▼ ▼ ▼

Five students—all with a different story. Each one somehow involved with the supernatural powers of darkness. For some it was a game. For others, it was a means of escape. And others saw it as a way to get the power necessary to change their situation in life.

Some of your friends may think this "Satan stuff" is all a big joke. Others may think it's cool to worship the devil.

What about you? Do you believe there is a spiritual battle raging today? Is the devil for real?

The best place we can go for answers is God's Word. The Bible describes the reality of spiritual warfare in Ephesians 6:12: "For our struggle is not against flesh and blood, but against the rulers, against the authorities, against the powers of this dark world and against the spiritual forces of evil in the heavenly realms."

There is evidence all around us today of this monumental spiritual battle. Just look at what is taking place on your campus, on the news, or in the broken families in your neighborhood. The devil is for real, he's our enemy, and he's playing for keeps. He and his troops are viciously attacking the kingdom of God. There will be no cease-fire or temporary truce.

Understanding the Battle

Even though our struggle is not against flesh and blood, the enemy still uses people and institutions. Satan has two great allies—the world system and the flesh. Spiritual warfare involves simultaneous action on all three battlefronts.

Satan's first ally is the world in which we live. Believers are warned not to love the world nor things in the world (1 John 2:15). We're challenged by materialism as well as a worldly philosophy that is contrary to everything God says. The attempts to lure us into a hostile position toward God come through the lust of the flesh, the lust of the eyes, and the boastful pride of life (1 John 2:16). The entire world is under the control of Satan (2 Corinthians 4:4; Ephesians 2:2).

The other ally of the enemy is the flesh. The term *flesh* refers to the human, physical dimension of our lives. It's the desire we all have to serve and please ourselves, to leave God out of our lives and live independent of Him (Romans 8:5,8; Ephesians 2:3). This capacity is still with us even after we become Christians, and if we're not careful it can cause a dullness in our lives to spiritual things.

So while Satan may not be directly involved when you are tempted to sin or enticed by the darkness, he certainly is the inspiration behind any temptation or enticement. He has constructed a massive web of evil to lure you away from God. You have the freedom of choice, though, so don't get caught up in extremes. Some people want to blame the devil for *everything*, and they see demons everywhere. The result is paranoia about the entire demonic world.

An equally dangerous extreme is not believing that Satan exists. If Satan can get you to believe a lie—like he doesn't exist—then he is able to do whatever he wants, and you'll never attribute it to him. You may have no idea that there is a spiritual battle going on for your soul, but that does not mean that the battle does not exist. Be alert! Satan is up to no good, and he will do everything in his power to defeat God's will for your life—even if it means you don't believe in him at all.

Deciding What We Are Going to Do

Once we understand the spiritual war, we must decide what we are going to do. How are we going to live in the world? How can we have victory over temptation? And ultimately, what does it mean to resist the devil?

The battle is real and we are all involved, like it or not. The only question is: Whose side are we fighting on? We cannot remain neutral. We must decide which kingdom we will stand for: right or wrong; heaven or hell; God or Satan.

I am convinced that teenagers are the number-one target of Satan. Does that surprise you? Scare you? I'm hoping it will motivate and challenge you to seriously consider what we'll be talking about in this book.

Satan already knows what the church needs to know: Teenagers are not just the future of this country and the world—they are the present as well. At the center of every major movement in history, you'll find teenagers. They have changed the course of history both for the good and the bad. And today, more than ever, I believe God is looking for students who are serious about making a difference for His kingdom.

You may just be dabbling with Satanism and the occult. Or you may be looking to strengthen your resources to stand firm against the enemy. Whatever your situation, this book is for you. We will be looking at the "battle for your mind," witchcraft, the New Age, why evil is so fascinating, how to be a candle in the dark, and more. And most important of all, you'll find some practical hands-on solutions to achieve victory in your life in the spiritual battle.

Study these pages carefully and apply what you learn. God wants *you* to be a beacon of light in your home, on your campus, and in your community. Let's prepare for battle!

Something to Think About

1. Have you or someone you know ever been involved in the occult or Satanism? How did you or this person get hooked?

2. What specific evidence indicates that spiritual warfare is real in your life? in your family? on your campus? in your neighborhood?

3. What is the greatest temptation you are currently struggling with in your life? How prepared do you feel to be able to resist the attacks of the enemy and his allies?

———————————

2

The Fascination with Evil

Audra got more than she bargained for when she followed the crowd at her high school. Witchcraft and Dungeons and Dragons are cool, her friends said. They also experimented with other fantasy role-playing games that had an evil slant. But it was okay, her friends said, because they were only playing games. Evil is just a state of mind. It wasn't hurting them.

The more Audra and her friends dabbled in evil, the more she became interested in wickedness.

One sleepless night she got up to grab a midnight snack. As she walked down the hallway toward the kitchen, she noticed a strange bright light in front of the refrigerator. Frightened, she heard a voice say to her, "Come into the light."

Fascinated by what she was seeing and hearing, Audra stepped into the light. Once inside, she saw two hallways in front of her—one was black and white, the other one green and red. Then she heard the voice again, only this time it was mocking her and laughing. Audra began to run through the colored hallways, looking for a way out. She kept taking wrong turns as she ran, going deeper and deeper into an endless maze of hallways.

Desperate to find a way of escape, she suddenly felt compelled to pray. Dropping to her knees, she cried out to God for help. When she got done praying, she opened her eyes and found herself back in the kitchen.

Later that week she met a guy at school named Billy, and she shared her experience with him. Billy suggested Audra talk to his pastor about it. When they got together, Billy's pastor spoke with Audra about the dangers of playing with evil—even though what she'd been doing seemed so innocent. He went on to explain that anything evil is offensive to God and causes harm to those involved. Audra realized that if she kept dabbling with evil, it would only cause more calamity in her life.

Was Audra's experience a bad dream, or did it really happen? Only God knows for sure. But if you were to ask Audra, she would say that it was very real to her, real enough to get her attention and cause her to make some changes in her life.

The Fascination with Evil

In the last few years there has been a tremendous rise in the preoccupation with evil and the occult throughout the world. Many young people today are like Audra—they are fascinated with things that are evil. They want to dabble and see what will happen if they do some wicked thing. It's like people are trying to see how close they can get to the fire without getting burned.

Some are enticed to play with evil because they're interested in forces and power greater than they are. They are looking for help to deal with the issues of life. Others find evil interesting and appealing because they are bored. Their lives lack meaning and purpose. They get up every day and go through the same routine with no goals or aspirations. Wickedness and the things of the occult can look pretty exciting. This fascination quickly turns into a growing appetite and eventually an obsession with the darkness. Most of the time things evolve so gradually, that these people don't even realize what they're getting into. Just like Audra, they slowly and subtly get sucked in, unaware of what is happening. No one wakes up one morning and suddenly decides to do something wicked.

But perhaps one of the most deceptive ways that evil can be appealing is when it's portrayed as fun and entertaining. Movies, cartoons, books, music, and games can sometimes have an element of wickedness that baits and hooks our curiosity. Such entertainment can appear to be funny, crazy, or even scary.

Take *Sin Magazine*, for example. Here's a publication designed for skaters and thrashers that is supposed to communicate the latest in art, music, culture, and the Scene. All this is done, however, with occultic artwork, articles encouraging rebellion and immoral sex, and voodoo comics. Or consider mega-selling author Stephen King's novels turned into movies, desensitizing millions to wickedness. When evil comes packaged in the form of entertainment or recreation, it disarms us to the dangers and the truth that we are playing with spiritual fire. And playing with fire can get you burned.

Where Evil Comes From

Have you ever wondered how you know when something is evil, and where evil came from? Webster's dictionary defines *evil* as that which is wicked, arising from bad character and causing discomfort or harm. In general, the Bible defines *evil* as being bad and harmful. *Bad* in the sense that doing something evil is disobeying God. And *harmful* due to the consequences experienced as a result of disobedience. To do evil is to be in opposition toward God, which is sin.

Evil came because of the freedom of choice. Evil was a necessary risk when God allowed people and angelic beings to have free wills. He knew there was the possibility of someone choosing to rebel against Him. And that is exactly what Satan did (Ezekiel 28:15).

We don't completely know why God allows evil, but we do know that He is able to bring glory to Himself through evil by expressing the grace and justice that are part of His character. Romans 9:22,23 puts it this way: "What if God, choosing to show his wrath and make his power known, bore with great patience the objects of his wrath—prepared for destruction? What if he did this to make the riches of his glory known to the objects of his mercy, whom he prepared in advance for glory?" By allowing evil and wickedness in our world, God can demonstrate His awesome love and care for each one of us.

The Bible teaches that the one behind all the wickedness in the world is Satan himself—the granddaddy of evil. Second Thessalonians 3:3 calls him the "evil one." Satan began his wicked work back with the very first man and woman.

While Adam and Eve were still sinless, they lived in paradise in a happy relationship with God. Then Satan, disguised as a serpent, tempted Eve with a lie and she disobeyed God. Adam also disobeyed as his wife had done and that resulted in their being banished from the Garden of Eden and separated from God (see Genesis 3). And ultimately, as a result of Adam and Eve's rebellion against God, sin entered the human race.

Because of Adam and Eve's choice to disobey God, you and I inherited this spiritual disease called *sin*. The Bible describes sin as rebellion against God (Joshua 1:17,18); knowing the right thing to do and not doing it (James 4:17); and missing the mark or standard that God has set before us (Romans 3:23).

And though this evil spiritual disease is worse than cancer or AIDS, having the potential to claim everyone's life, there is a cure. Romans 5:8 says, "But God demonstrates his own love for us in this: While we were still sinners, Christ died for us." The antidote for sin is found in a personal relationship with Jesus. That's the good news.

The Conflict with the World and the Flesh

In Chapter 1 I mentioned that spiritual warfare involves more than just Satan and his demonic forces of darkness. It also includes our battle with the world and the flesh. The devil's evil influence, though, can be seen in both these battlefronts.

The world system is headed by Satan, which leaves God out and is a rival to Him. The values and the attitudes that characterize this system are the lust of the flesh, the lust of the eyes, and the boastful pride of life (1 John 2:16). When Satan tempted Eve, he tempted her in these three areas (Genesis 3:6). When the devil tempted Jesus in the wilderness, these were also the three areas of attack (Matthew 4:1-11).

The lust of the flesh is the preoccupation with gratifying physical cravings and desires. A great example of this today is the incredible overemphasis on sex in our society. Have you noticed how sex sells everything from cars to vitamins? Everywhere we turn we are bombarded with sexually explicit messages on TV, in movies, and in music. Of course, lust of the flesh doesn't have to be sexual. It can also be an out-of-control desire for food or a self-sufficient attitude that says, "I don't need God to satisfy my cravings."

The lust of the eyes, or materialism, is the unchecked desire to accumulate things. We live in a society that is loaded with temptations in this area. Ad slogans tell us that we deserve to have a particular product or way of life, or we should get all we can get *now* because we only go around once in life. How about the new car commercials or the ads for the latest fashion? Guaranteed to make you feel that what you currently own is somehow not good enough. While there's nothing wrong with admiring nice things, it becomes a problem when it goes from appreciation to a "must have" mentality.

The boastful pride of life is being obsessed with one's status or importance. Finding your identity in what you do on the football field or how well you sing or even who your family is can be a trap. Isn't it amazing how far people will go to feel important or to gain status? Just look at the gang problem. Students are doing crazy, illegal, and sometimes deadly things to belong to a local gang. Defining ourselves in terms of our achievements, our position, or our success will never bring lasting security, acceptance, or fulfillment.

The things of the world won't last. We are told not to love these things because they are not from God. And if the weaknesses of our human flesh are left unchecked, patterns can develop that can be deadly to our spiritual well-being. God values self-control (not the lust of the flesh), a spirit of generosity (not the lust of the eyes), and humble service (not the boastful pride of life). When Satan attacks with these temptations, focus in on contentment and where it comes from. Learn to not only say no, but also to be satisfied with who you are and what you have.

The apostle Paul put it this way:

> I am not saying this because I am in need, for I have learned to be content whatever the circumstances. I know what it is to be in need, and I know what it is to have plenty. I have learned the secret of being content in any and every situation, whether well fed or hungry, whether living in plenty or in want. I can do

everything through him who gives me strength (Philippians 4:11-13).

The key is to trust God and depend on Him for direction in every dimension of your life. But sometimes it's easy to think that you have it pretty well together, and you don't need to consult God in a certain area of your life. I wish I could say I've never been caught in that trap, but I have. Maybe you can relate.

A Close Call

I was a new Christian and convinced that God wanted to use me to win my former high school sweetheart to Christ. After several years without contact she had sent me a note suggesting that we get together during the Christmas holidays. *This is it,* I thought. *We can get back together and fall in love. She will give her life to Jesus, and everything will be great.*

There was just one problem with my plan. I was leaving God totally out of the picture. I had decided I could handle this one on my own. God had other more important things to deal with—like running the universe. Some friends in the college group at church warned me repeatedly about the dangers of ignoring God's desires for this area of my life. They told me to consider what the Bible says concerning dating non-Christians. They felt my motive in wanting my ex-girlfriend to come to Christ was good, but cautioned me that oftentimes it is easier for a Christian to get pulled down into a compromising situation than to pull the lost person up—especially in a dating situation.

On the first night back together everything started out fine, until we went to dinner. In the restaurant I noticed that she had become a heavy smoker and liked alcohol an awful lot. She invited me to participate. I knew what God's

Word said about things like this, yet I began to rationalize the need to make her feel comfortable. I concluded that a little bit wouldn't hurt me.

Then she invited me over to her apartment to look at our old yearbooks and pictures from things we did together. It seemed innocent enough to me, and I figured it would be a good chance to tell her about the Lord (so far He hadn't fit comfortably in our conversation). Once at her place she began to close the drapes and said she wanted to change into something more comfortable to "give me a night I would never forget."

All of a sudden it was as if someone grabbed me by the shirt and picked me up. I told her I had to go, then walked out the door and drove away. I never saw her again. When I look back on the situation, I realize God spared me the pain of compromise and disobedience to the standards of His Word. I was very fortunate that the Lord rescued me from giving in to the temptation that Satan had attacked me with. Who knows what the consequences might have been for leaving God out of this dimension of my life? The results could have been disastrous.

As I have grown in my relationship with the Lord, I have come to realize that God wants to be part of every area of my life, no matter how small and insignificant I might think it is. I've learned the importance of making biblically based choices and considering the consequences of my decisions. And I've also learned that the devil will often tempt us with things that look good but are designed to sidetrack us and keep us from experiencing God's best for our lives.

If we are to respond to God in the way He desires and live the quality of life that He has designed for us, we must stop acting based on motives that reflect the world's value system. Make sure to check the heavenly loyalty of your heart and the focus of your mind. And as you do this, follow the advice in 1 Thessalonians 5:22, "Avoid every kind of evil."

Be alert. Satan is up to no good. He will do everything in his power to defeat God's will for your life. And he doesn't always approach everyone in the same way. What is temptation for one person may or may not be a problem for someone else. I'd like to conclude this chapter by telling you about a guy named Mark David Chapman. For him, the fascination with evil revolved around his search for power, eventually becoming an opening for Satan's influence in his life. And it had disastrous results.

The Search for Power

It was the early sixties, when the Beatles' popularity exploded in America. Mark David Chapman's family lived in Decatur, Georgia, where his father gave Mark his first rock-'n'-roll album, "Meet the Beatles." Like millions of fans in America, nine-year-old Mark immediately fell under the spell of Beatlemania and would be influenced dramatically by their music until he was an adult.

Mark was a very lonely child who would often escape into a world of imaginary people. According to Chapman, he had hundreds of thousands of them living in the walls of his bedroom, and he was their king. It was his way of coping with an abusive father.

When Mark was 14, the Beatles released "Magical Mystery Tour," an album filled with drug-inspired imagery. Mark eagerly entered into the world of LSD until finding a direction for his life, several years later, working with refugees as a YMCA camp counselor. Everyone thought he was terrific, including his staff of 15.

When the camp closed down, he decided to go to college. He went from being a big man at camp to a nobody on campus—the same kind of nobody he was when he was a little kid. Severe depression took over Mark's life. He dropped out of college and bought a one-way ticket to Hawaii to kill himself.

After buying a cheap piece of plastic vacuum cleaner hose at Sears, he found a supposedly deserted spot on the north shore of the island. He hooked up the hose to the exhaust and sat in the car after turning it on. But he was discovered by some people and saved.

After a few weeks in the hospital he was released, got a job, and met a travel agent named Gloria. He and Gloria fell in love and were married, but the honeymoon was quickly over as Gloria watched this quiet, gentle man turn into a violent, unpredictable stranger. When Mark got frustrated he would grab his wife and hit her, just as his father did with his mother.

Mark seemed to be struggling to find himself. He drifted from job to job and was moody. Deep down inside he was losing his grip on reality. At the same time he became obsessed with the book *The Catcher in the Rye*, the story of a teenager who leaves school on a three-day journey to find himself. After looking in various places in Manhattan, the main character of the book doesn't find anything but a bunch of phoniness.

Chapman assumed the identity of the fictional teenager in the book and became a believer in the character's campaign against phoniness. One day while visiting his only peaceful oasis, the public library, Mark came across a book about John Lennon from the Beatles called *One Day at a Time*. As he looked at the pictures he began judging Lennon, especially after learning Lennon lived in a very expensive and exclusive co-op called The Dakota in Manhattan. This angered Chapman because he felt Lennon had sold out on the Beatles' earlier idealism.

In Mark David Chapman's disturbed mind the pieces were falling into place. Though he felt like a king-sized nobody, he saw this real somebody as a phony. Suddenly his nobody was wanting to strike down this somebody.

Mark bought a .38 pistol and a plane ticket to New York City. When he checked out of his maintenance job for the last time, he signed out as "John Lennon." He went to New York's Central Park to prepare to eliminate this phony somebody. In a television interview later, Chapman said that before he killed John Lennon, he turned to Satan because he knew he wouldn't have the strength to kill a man on his own.[1] He went through what he thought was an appropriate satanic ritual and took off all his clothes and chanted and screamed and howled. "I asked Satan to give me the power to kill John Lennon," Chapman said.[2] He shot and killed John Lennon in front of The Dakota apartments. He was sentenced to 20 years to life in prison.

Mark David Chapman went searching for power to help him accomplish something that would give him a sense of significance. He claims he found it in Satan. In some ways, Mark is no different than a lot of people today who are looking for a source of power to help them deal with the pain of life.

Power is an interesting concept. It can create havoc and corrupt someone if it is obtained from the wrong source and abused, as it was with Mark. It is alluring because it is a means of control, authority, or influence over others. I've talked with a number of students who say the power they have gotten from Satan makes them feel special. It gives them a sense of significance among their friends.

The Bible speaks much about power. The power of Jesus Christ is described as supreme (Ephesians 1:19-21), unlimited (Matthew 28:18), everlasting (1 Timothy 6:16), and able to subdue all things (Philippians 3:21). It is demonstrated in Jesus rising from the dead (John 2:19-22), overcoming the world (John 16:33), overcoming Satan (Colossians 2:15), and destroying the works of Satan (1 John 3:8).

Satan's power is a counterfeit. It's limited, temporary, and designed to lure people away from trusting God. Our source of power comes from God. Isaiah 40:29-31 says, "He gives strength to the weary and increases the power of the weak. Even youths grow tired and weary, and young men stumble and fall; but those who hope in the LORD will renew their strength. They will soar on wings like eagles; they will run and not grow weary, they will walk and not be faint." The key to obtaining this power is to put our hope in God and not the things of this world. The same power that raised Jesus from the grave is available to you and me to help us face the challenges of life. Access to this power is granted when we receive Christ as our Savior and Lord.

We live in an evil and seductive world. But God has equipped us with every resource necessary to win the battles we face from the darkness. Second Timothy 1:7 says, "For God did not give us a spirit of timidity, but a spirit of power, of love and of self-discipline." If you really want to experience victory over the darkness, you must stop opening yourself up to every weird value and attitude that the world puts in your path. The Bible says we must turn from evil and do good (1 Peter 3:11).

God has given us all the resources we need through His Son, His Spirit, prayer, and the Bible to help us avoid every form of evil in our lives. When we are bored, tempted, or need help and power to overcome the difficulties of life, we need to turn to Christ. He should be our first resource, not our last resort. The security, acceptance, and significance we need to win in life is found in Jesus.

So stop being fascinated with evil, and start getting absorbed with God!

Something to Think About

1. How do you most frequently come in conflict with the world? What do you need to do so you won't be so vulnerable to this temptation?

2. Have you ever been tempted to leave God out of a situation in your life? What happened?

3. What insights did you gain from the story of Mark David Chapman's search for power? What kind of power do you think most young people are searching for today?

4. How would you describe your relationship with Christ right now? How do you think He would describe your relationship with Him?

3

Do You Know
Your Enemy?

At 5:30 the evening before Thanksgiving the phone rang at my office. Dan, a deputy and a good friend, was calling from the sheriff's station. "Steve," he said, "can you give me five minutes?"

"What's up?" I asked.

Dan explained that they had just picked up a 15-year-old girl in a convenience store who had tried to kill herself with a steak knife. "We're going to place her in protective custody at a local hospital," he said. "But you gotta talk to her. She really needs help."

Jennifer got on the phone and said she wanted to kill herself because no one cared. She had been abandoned by her parents and had been living in a series of foster homes for most of her life. "I just can't take the loneliness and pain anymore," she said.

I tried to tell her that I cared about her and wanted to help.

"No you don't," she said. "You don't even know me."

Realizing our conversation was getting nowhere fast, I decided to change my tactics. "Jennifer," I asked, "do you know where you'll go when you die?"

"Absolutely," she responded. "I'm going straight to hell."

"Is that really where you want to go?" I questioned.

"Yes," she said. "And I want to go there as soon as I can."

"Jennifer, there is another option—another place where you can spend eternity," I explained.

"Oh, I suppose you're going to tell me about the lies of heaven," she said sarcastically.

"Who told you that heaven was a lie?" I asked.

"My god."

"Who is your god?"

"Satan," Jennifer replied. "And he would never lie to me."

I desperately tried to explain to her the lies of Satan and the love Jesus had for her. "Call me when you get to the hospital," I pleaded. "I really do want to help you."

With a coldness in her voice she responded, "Is that all you have to say?"

"Just remember, Jennifer, Jesus loves you," I said. With that she hung up the phone, and I never heard from her again.

Jennifer is like many students today who have listened to the wrong voice and bought Satan's big lie. They may not all have tried to kill themselves, but they are vulnerable to the subtle seduction of the enemy's attacks.

We are involved in a battle for our very souls. It is a war between the kingdom of light and the kingdom of darkness. Between the kingdom of right and the kingdom of wrong. Between the kingdom of God and the kingdom of Satan.

For us to fully grasp this spiritual warfare, we must first understand the strategy and tactics of our enemy.

The Reality of Satan

Satan has done a masterful job at confusing us about his true identity. Plenty of movies, books, games, song lyrics, and celebrities represent Satan as other than he truly is. It is so easy to get the wrong idea about Satan and, in the process, lose sight of the intensity of the spiritual battle.

We see Satan usually portrayed in one of two ways in the world. Sometimes he is pictured as a goofy little buffoon, wearing a red suit with horns on top of his head, carrying a strange-looking pitchfork, running around poking people. I see this every Halloween in our neighborhood. Little kids trick-or-treat dressed up as the devil in these red polyester suits, carrying a plastic pitchfork.

Satan is also portrayed in the other extreme: as a horrible-looking creature that is part human, part monster, and part alien, with bulging eyes, fire for breath, and the most hideously evil laugh imaginable. Stephen King novels and slasher movies are filled with these images, and even CD covers and comic books depict the enemy in this way.

Satan has used these and other imaginative pictures of himself to confuse us and disarm us. It's no wonder so many people today don't take him seriously. Satan's strategy is working all too well.

In a national survey,[1] the question was asked, "Is the devil for real?" Of those who responded, 43 percent who claimed to be born-again Christians said no, that Satan was just a symbol of evil. Satan would like nothing better than for people, especially those of us who are Christians, to be deceived into believing that he doesn't exist. After all, if Satan isn't for real, we don't have to be concerned about spiritual warfare. And so we lose.

That's why it's important to rely on what the Bible says. The world will give us confusing information when it comes to spiritual things. God's Word is the ultimate source of truth. The Bible confirms the reality of Satan and gives us an accurate picture of his true character.

In Ezekiel 28 we learn much about Satan. Let's look at just a few verses from this chapter. In verse 12 we read, "You were the model of perfection, full of wisdom and perfect in beauty." Verse 15 says, "You were blameless in your ways from the day you were created till wickedness was found in you." Then in verse 17 we read, "Your heart became proud on account of your beauty, and you corrupted your wisdom because of your splendor. So I threw you to the earth; I made a spectacle of you before kings."

Satan is the wisest and most beautiful being ever created, but he can only go and do as far as God permits. Nothing else in all creation could compare to him, yet he made a horrible choice to rebel against God, ultimately plunging all of creation into a deadly spiritual war.

Satan's incredible pride led him to rebel against God. He refused to accept the fact that all of his greatness came from God. As his pride grew, he determined to take over God's kingdom and seize control of His power. Satan, the most beautiful, the most powerful, and the wisest of all created beings, started a war he could never win.

Because of His awesome holiness, God could not tolerate rebellion and evil in His kingdom. He stripped Satan of his position of authority, drove him from heaven, and made a disgrace of him as he threw him to earth. Though this battle between God and Satan started in heaven, we are now caught right in the middle of it on earth. And because of Satan's great hatred and anger toward God, he is not about to let us walk away untouched by his fierce attacks.

The Character of Satan

Now that we know more about Satan's true identity, it will also be helpful to know more about his character— what he's like. Even though Satan in his present fallen state retains a great deal of power, he still has limitations.

The names given to Satan provide us with insight into

his characteristics, background, and activities. Here's a brief look at the names of Satan, their meaning, and some of the passages where you can find this particular name used.

Name	Meaning	Passage
Satan	Adversary/opposer	Zechariah 3:1; Matthew 4:10; Revelation 12:9; 20:2
Devil	Slanderer	Matthew 4:1; Ephesians 4:27
Evil one	Intrinsically evil	John 17:15; 1 John 5:18,19
Serpent	Craftiness	Genesis 3:1; 2 Corinthians 11:3
Ancient serpent	Deceiver in Eden	Revelation 12:9
Dragon	Fierce nature	Revelation 12:3,7,9
Abaddon	Destruction	Revelation 9:11
Apollyon	Destroyer	Revelation 9:11
Enemy	Opponent	1 Peter 5:8
Accuser of the brothers	Opposes believers before God	Revelation 12:10
Tempter	Entices people to sin	Matthew 4:3; 1 Thessalonians 3:5
Prince of this world	Rules in world system	John 12:31
The spirit who is now at work in those who are disobedient		Ephesians 2:2
Beelzebub	Chief of the demons	Luke 11:15

Name	Meaning	Passage
Belial	Worthlessness/ wickedness	2 Corinthians 6:15
God of this age	Controls philosophy of the world	2 Corinthians 4:4
Ruler of the kingdom of the air	Control of unbelievers	Ephesians 2:2
Father of lies	Perverts the truth	John 8:44
Murderer	Leads people to eternal death	John 8:44
Angel of light		2 Corinthians 11:14

Satan is also described in 1 Peter 5:8 as a roaring lion, looking for someone to devour. You might say that he is like a serial killer stalking his next victim. But if we know Christ, there is no reason to live in constant fear of what Satan may do next. God has not given us a spirit of fear, but rather one of power (2 Timothy 1:7). First John 4:4 tells us that greater is He that is in us than he that is in the world. Satan is a created being; he is no match for God. When we know Christ as our Savior, we can have victory over the attacks of the devil.

The Strategies of Satan

Because Satan was created above all others in intelligence, he is a brilliant war planner and has developed some deceptive strategies to use in his attacks against us. Part of his overall plan includes: doubt, difficulties, self-sufficiency, false teaching, and confusion. Let's take a closer look at each one of these tactics.

Doubt

Satan wants to undermine God's character and credibility. He started this back in the Garden of Eden with Adam and Eve. Satan wanted them to doubt what God said and why He said it (Genesis 3). In turn, the devil wants us to be uncertain of who God is and what He is like. Satan would also like us to be skeptical about the promises of God's Word and even doubt that we know Him. Satan will do all he can to make us ineffective through doubt.

The Bible clearly says that Satan is a liar (John 8:44) and that God is incapable of lying (Titus 1:2). When you struggle with doubt, think of evidence in the past of God's faithfulness to you and others you know or have read about in the Bible. Get your eyes off any circumstances that may be causing you to doubt, and put your eyes on the Lord. Make sure you saturate your heart and mind in God's Word (Romans 10:17). If you're dealing with doubt, here are some other verses you can look at: Psalm 14:1; John 10:28; and James 1:5-8.

Difficulties

The devil will use difficulties and problems in your life to make things hard—stress at home with your parents, pressure on campus with friends, sometimes different forms of persecution on the job. Satan's adversity may even come from individuals within your youth group at church. He tries anything and everything to frustrate God's plan for your life. Ultimately, the enemy would like you to get so discouraged that you turn your back on God.

When the going gets tough, remember what Jesus said in John 16:33: "I have told you these things, so that in me you may have peace. In this world you will have trouble. But take heart! I have overcome the world." No matter how bad things may get, Jesus promises to never leave us or turn His back on us (Hebrews 13:5). Instead of asking God why these things may be happening to you, ask Him how He wants to help you through this difficult time in your life. Here are some additional thoughts from God's Word to look at: John 15:18-20 and Romans 16:20.

Self-Sufficiency

Satan wants us to trust in our own strength and resources and not to rely on God. He works hard at misleading us to place our confidence in the wrong things. This is sometimes reinforced by the messages we hear in the world, those philosophies that go exactly opposite of what the Bible says: "Be all that you can be," "You've come a long way," "The power is within you." The list goes on and on. The devil works subtly to keep us just slightly off track, making us think we can live independent of God.

You'll know that this tactic is working in your life when your prayer life becomes almost nonexistent and your time in God's Word disintegrates into nothing. Self-reliance is really what the very core of sin is—living independent of God. Satan wants us to rely on ourselves and not on the resurrection power of Jesus Christ.

God wants us to rely on Him for everything, and He promises to provide. The Bible teaches in John 15:5, "Apart from me you can do nothing." When you need answers or have challenges in your life to overcome, depend on God. The apostle Paul wrote, "I can do everything through him who gives me strength" (Philippians 4:13). How about you? Are you tempted to rely on your own strength rather than God's? Check out these verses for more help: Psalm 84:5 and Proverbs 3:5,6.

False Teaching

The devil wants to frustrate and mislead us with false teaching. You may know some well-meaning people who are members of false religions or cults (Mormons or Jehovah's Witnesses, for example) who teach that Jesus was just a good man. Other groups say that Jesus is here on earth, leading them. Sometimes, listening to false teaching can be deadly. Look at what happened in Waco, Texas. More than 80 people, including children, followed cult leader David Koresh to his death because he said he was God. I believe most of those people would be alive today if they knew their Bible better and recognized the lies of the enemy.

The problem is that we have very subtly strayed from the teaching of God's Word. We rely more on what people say rather than what God says. We are not spending enough time studying the Bible, so we don't know how to respond to the issues of life from God's perspective. We are easily led astray.

The primary way God communicates to us is through His written Word. One of the marks of growth in your spiritual life is finding yourself turning to the Bible more frequently in your search for answers. Don't neglect time alone in God's Word. We'll talk more about this in Part 3, but in the meantime here are some verses to look at: Luke 6:47 and 2 Timothy 3:16.

Confusion

The devil is a master at confusing us with mixed messages. Satan has worked hard at eroding society's standards, making morality look old-fashioned and outdated and immorality cool. Whether dealing with sex, drugs, or alcohol, the messages can be pretty confusing: "Just do it," "Just say no," "Just wear a condom," "Just make it safe."

Satan wants us to be so baffled about what is right and what is wrong that we will compromise our faith in Christ. When our life is in a blur, it is much easier for him to mislead us. Living in a confusing world like ours can be dangerous to our spiritual health. Isaiah 5:20 puts it this way: "Woe to those who call evil good and good evil, who put darkness for light and light for darkness, who put bitter for sweet and sweet for bitter."

When you are feeling confused, just remember that God is not a God of confusion but a God of peace (1 Corinthians 14:33). Take time to ask God for wisdom and direction for your situation. Pray and then examine God's Word for wisdom. Here are some places to get started: Isaiah 30:21 and Philippians 4:6,7.

The Reality of Demons

The Bible reminds us that the spiritual battle includes not only Satan but his demons as well. Without question the Bible affirms the reality of demons. Jesus confirms the existence of demons numerous times during His earthly ministry (Matthew 10:1; 12:22-28; 15:22-28; Mark 5:1-16; Luke 10:17). All the writers of the New Testament (except Hebrews) mention demons. There are also many passages in the Old Testament where demons are referred to.

Demons are more than just figures of speech, cosmic forces, or concepts that merely exist in our minds. They are spirit beings (Ephesians 6:12). They are not present everywhere, but they are not so restricted as human beings by the normal barriers of space.

Demons possess intelligence (Mark 1:24), emotions (Luke 8:28; James 2:19), wills (Luke 8:32), and personality (Luke 8:27-30). They can also possess superhuman strength at times, like the demon-possessed man in Mark 5:1-16. Having chosen to rebel against God with Satan, demons continue to oppose the purposes of God in this world. They promote false religion (1 John 4:1-4; 1 Timothy 4:1-3) and the worship of idols (Leviticus 17:7; Deuteronomy 32:17; 1 Corinthians 10:20).

Satan's identity, his various names, his cohorts, and his strategies not only affirm the reality of his existence but also reveal his many-faceted character and the aspects of his work. He is a powerful, intelligent, and clever creature. We must never underestimate our enemy or his forces of darkness. He has a plan and a purpose for everyone. For those without Christ, he will do all he can to keep them from receiving Jesus as Savior and Lord of their lives. He doesn't care how much people go to church, youth group activities, or Christian concerts—just as long as they don't open their hearts to Christ. And his plan for those who have established that all-important relationship is to keep them from growing in the strength and knowledge of following Jesus as a disciple, and from telling others how they can find new life in Christ.

In spite of all this, the good news is ours: Jesus is our defender and He defeated Satan on the cross at Calvary. Colossians 2:15 tells us that Jesus disarmed the powers and authorities, making a spectacle of them and triumphing over them by the cross. The devil is powerless in the presence of the Son of God. Ultimately, Satan will be judged and cast into the lake of fire for eternity (Revelation 20:7-10).

We are on the winning side with Christ as our Savior. God has given us all the necessary resources to withstand the attacks of the enemy, including special spiritual weaponry and equipment. Our strategy for victory is summed up in James 4:7: "Submit yourselves, then, to God. Resist the devil, and he will flee from you." We'll be talking more about the help that God has given us in Part 3, "Standing Up to the Devil."

Something to Think About

1. Have you ever known anyone like Jennifer who was deeply involved in the occult? How could you help someone like that?

2. What strategy does the devil most often use in your life? Why? What does God want you to do in this situation to achieve victory?

3. List some specific examples of confusing messages you have noticed in the world. How can you best prepare yourself to be on guard against these subtle attacks?

4

The Battle for Your Mind

Star Tours is a fascinating ride. It's the only place I know where the average person can board a "shuttle craft" and take a flight through "space." I still remember the first time I rode it at Disneyland. What an experience! The moment I got in line, vivid pictures around me prepared me for the ride. The longer I stood in line, the more things I saw (and believe me, it was a long wait in line!). To my right there was a thrashed spacecraft with R2D2 and C-3PO working on it. In front of me a screen was flashing a flight schedule, telling me when the next spacecraft was going to take off and its destination. Above the flight schedule an even bigger screen showed moving pictures of shuttle crafts flying to distant planets. And the noise! R2D2 and C-3PO were arguing with each other, some alien kept making announcements over the PA system, ads for tours to other planets played every few seconds, and alarms constantly went off.

My mind started playing tricks on me. Was this just a ride at an amusement park or was I really going to outer space? One look at the long line of people behind me woke me up to reality—or so I thought!

When I finally reached the entrance of the spacecraft, the doors quickly opened and I grabbed a seat. The flight attendant announced our departure and asked us to "Please fasten your seat belt." Something clicked in my mind, and I snapped the seat belt into place. For the next few minutes I *know* I went into hyperspace. My stomach was up in my throat as I hung on. All of a sudden we screeched to a halt and the ride was over. And though I never left the room, never went more than two or three feet the whole time I was on the ride, my mind told me that I had just returned from a trip to outer space.

Our mind is an amazing thing. There is no computer in the world that can match its capabilities. But just like a computer, the mind needs to have "software" installed to enable us to function. Most of us spend at least 12 years of our life getting an education—installing "software" into our minds at school. But we also receive data from the music we listen to, the movies and television we watch, and the books and magazines we read. All of the things we store in our mind are eventually going to make their way out at some time in the things we do and say. What goes in is going to influence the way we live.

For example, think about the commercials you see on TV, especially the ones advertising food. You're spread out on the couch, watching your favorite show, when Bill Cosby pops on the screen with a bowl of Jell-O instant pudding—and man, does it look good! Your mind sends a signal to your stomach that you need to have some Jell-O pudding, and it doesn't matter that you just ate 20 minutes ago. You are suddenly motivated to do something based on what you have seen on the tube. That's what advertising is designed to do. And it starts in the mind.

It all begins with what goes in. The information comes from a variety of directions—school, TV, videos, etc. Once you let something into your mind through your eyes or ears, it begins to shape your thoughts. Thoughts then begin to form attitudes. Ultimately attitudes determine behavior. Do you see the process? It is really simple.

Do you ever wonder why you do some of the things that you do? Perhaps you need to take a look at the things you are allowing to come into your mind. The Bible explains it in this way: "But the things that come out of the mouth come from the heart, and these make a man 'unclean.' For out of the heart come evil thoughts, murder, adultery, sexual immorality, theft, false testimony, slander" (Matthew 15:18,19). The word *heart*, in this case, stands for a person's entire mental and moral activity. In other words, it pictures the inward personal life—mind and emotions. Because sin takes a seat in the center of our inward life, it can short-circuit our actions, as mentioned in these verses.

If a commercial can motivate us to buy something, is it possible that seeing something in a movie, reading a comic book, or listening to a CD could influence our thinking in such a way as to cause us to do something. Maybe something that is violent and harmful to ourselves or others. Think about it.

Nineteen-year-old Mark Branch killed himself after stabbing an 18-year-old female college student to death. When the cops searched his room, they found 90 horror movies as well as a machete and a goalie mask like those used by Jason, the grisly star of *Friday the 13th*.[1]

Or what about the nine-year-old boy who sprayed a Bronx office building with gunfire? The boy explained to an astonished police sergeant how he learned to load his Uzi-style gun: "I watch a lot of TV."[2]

Obviously these are extreme cases, and there are other factors that need to be considered in each situation, but you can't deny the connection with violence in the media and its effect on the mind. Researchers in all walks of the social sciences have studied the question of whether TV and other forms of media entertainment cause violence. The results have been incredibly conclusive. Numerous groups over the years have called for curbing violence. Even some video game manufacturers have started to put warning labels on certain cartridges.

And what about other problems challenging students today, like drug and alcohol abuse or premarital sex? While there are other contributing factors to these problems, including the breakdown of the family, if you look carefully, you will see a direct connection between the increase in these problems and the change in our entertainment values in this country in the last 30 years. And the mind is the key player in the midst of it all.

The heat of the spiritual battle is taking place between our ears. That's where the war is going to be won or lost. The Bible says much about the mind, and one of the key principles is that how a person thinks, so he or she is (see Proverbs 23:7). In other words, what we think about all day long is what we are going to become. Our minds are like a blank slate, waiting to be written on. That's why it is critical to learn to filter the information we are allowing into our mind. (We'll talk more about how to do this in Part 3 in a chapter called "Take Control.")

The apostle Paul wrote that before we were Christians, we were separated from God and were enemies in our minds because of our evil behavior (Colossians 1:21). Because of sin, the mind is an enemy of God. Without Christ, our minds can be controlled by all kinds of wicked thoughts. The Bible also says that a person can have a blinded mind. In 2 Corinthians 4:4 we read that the god of this world— Satan—has blinded the minds of unbelievers so they can-not see the light of the gospel. In other words, when the message of God's love is presented, the devil conceals it from an unbeliever's mind. However, the Holy Spirit can break through these tactics of the enemy.

The Bible also warns believers not to be deceived by the cunningness of the devil, who wants to lead our minds away from sincere and pure devotion to Christ (2 Corinthians 11:3). How can the enemy hope to accomplish this? By influencing our thinking through using what we put into our mind.

What are you filling your mind with? It's amazing what is available. I just received an offer in the mail from a computer software company. One of the highlighted selling features of this software is the ability to program personal subliminal messages. While you work on your computer, little messages flash periodically on the screen that you will not fully be conscious of but that will be programming your mind with whatever you want. And computers are just one of many ways our minds can gather information.

Who or What We Are Battling

This battle raging to control and influence our thinking is coming from the same three major sources we looked at briefly in Chapter 1, "Satan's Targets."

The Flesh

We are all born with a desire to live independent of God. This desire comes from our sin nature or flesh. This nature has been passed down through the generations from Adam and Eve to every person except Jesus. We were born as slaves to sin, or the flesh (Romans 6:6,17). The power of this wicked hold that the flesh has over each one of us is broken when we accept Christ (Romans 6:18). But even though the power of sin over us is broken, our flesh is still tempted by the forces of darkness and the philosophies of the world system.

The flesh is by far the most influential enemy facing the Christian (Romans 8:1-17; Galatians 3:3; Ephesians 2:3). It's what gives our other two enemies the chance to operate in our minds.

The World

This enemy is not the physical planet we live on, but has more to do with a way of thinking. Many times in the New Testament, the world is presented as something hostile to God (John 17:14; 18:36; 1 Corinthians 3:19; 1 John 2:15-17). Worldly ideas that influence thinking seem to change with every generation. At the heart of this worldly thinking is always a stirring up of the flesh to indulge in a variety of sins. And often this worldliness is presented in a beautiful way. Despite the appeal of worldly philosophies, we have the power through Christ not to give in to the enticement.

The Devil

The last chapter dealt with Satan, the god of this world, so I won't take time to repeat what we already looked at. But remember, the devil will use any type of attractive or not-so-attractive ideas, concepts, methods, or attitudes to influence our thinking and tempt us to live independent of God. Yet God has made it possible for each one of us to win the war for our mind against this enemy.

Power vs. Truth

Satan is not only a clever enemy, but an intelligent one as well. In Chapter 3 we learned that the devil was created above all others in intelligence. He knows all too well that the key to victory in the spiritual battle for our mind is *truth* rather than power. Let me explain.

I have met some well-meaning Christians who somehow have the misconception that God has recruited them to be devil busters—to go around kicking the devil in the rump! As exciting as it may sound to be a Rambo for Righteousness, it's not biblical. Nowhere in God's Word will you find that some kind of spiritual power confrontation with the forces of darkness will set you free. God does not want us running around picking fights with the devil and his demons.

Instead we are to stand firm, resist the devil, and he will flee from us (Ephesians 6:13,14; James 4:7). Victory and freedom will come when we confront the powers of darkness with the truth. And what is truth? Basically, truth means that the facts conform to reality; truth identifies things as they are.

The facts are that Satan is a liar; he distorts and twists the truth. There is no truth in him (John 8:44). He is a deceiver and works subtly to mislead us. He knows that if he can get us to believe a lie, we will live the lie. Here's a sample of some of the more common lies he uses with students today:

- Money will make you happy.
- Sex is okay, as long as it's safe.
- Looks are everything.
- It's okay to drink, just don't drive.
- Follow the crowd and you are never alone.

- Live for today and don't worry about tomorrow.
- You are a product of evolution.
- You will never make it or be successful.
- There are no consequences for the choices you make.
- God has a lousy plan for your life.

Satan's power is in the lie, but the devil doesn't have a leg to stand on when we confront him with the truth of God and His Word. God is reliable and He cannot lie (Titus 1:2; Hebrews 6:18). The Bible exposes Satan and his lies for what they really are. Satan wants us to fear him more than we fear God. When the devil's lie is exposed by truth, his plans are defeated.

If the devil's power is in the lie, then our power as believers is in knowing the truth. But how can we know and understand the truth? Through knowing God and studying and living out His Word in our daily lives.

Jesus said that when you know the truth, the truth will set you free (John 8:32). He also said that He was the way, the truth, and the life (John 14:6). Jesus' death and resurrection defeated and disarmed the rulers and authorities of the kingdom of darkness (Colossians 2:15). In Christ we have the freedom to live as God designed us to live. The first thing we need to do is to establish a relationship with Jesus Christ. (If you haven't already done that, then take a few minutes right now and turn to the chapter "Freedom from the Power of Darkness" in Part 3.)

Once we receive Christ, God sends His Spirit to live within us and to guide us into all truth (John 16:13). God promises to keep us from the evil one by teaching us His words of truth (John 17:15,17). His words of truth are found in the Bible. Our responsibility as believers is to let our mind dwell on what is true (Philippians 4:8). How do we practically do this?

By understanding who we are in Christ and by using God's Word as a filter for what we feed our mind on, comparing everything we see, read, or hear to what the Bible teaches. This will enable us to choose the truth over a lie. Many believers today are living defeated lives because they don't know what the Bible teaches, so they can't expose the devil's lies with the truth. Remember, if you don't spend consistent, quality time in God's Word, you make yourself vulnerable to the influence of Satan's lies.

And don't think that, just because you're a Christian, Satan is no longer interested in manipulating your life through your mind. He knows that if he can direct your thoughts, he can ultimately direct your behavior. Satan's objective is to tempt you to live independent of God. The Bible teaches that the devil can put thoughts in our mind. Just look at how he influenced the following people.

In 1 Chronicles 21:1, David sinned by counting his fighting men when God had told him specifically not to. John 13:2 says that the devil prompted Judas to betray Jesus. And in Acts 5:3 Peter confronts Ananias, "How is it that Satan has so filled your heart that you have lied to the Holy Spirit and have kept for yourself some of the money you received for the land?"

Be careful to guard your thoughts. Don't allow Satan to influence your behavior.

Satan's Battle with Teenagers

What thoughts is Satan infiltrating your mind with? I wrote a book for parents on protecting kids from Satanism, the New Age, and the occult. In doing research for the book, my coauthor and I surveyed several thousand students across the country in Christian settings—Christian camps, schools, and churches.[3] Before I give you the results, I want you to take the survey yourself and then you can compare your answers with the other responses. Answer yes or no to the following questions:

1. Have you ever experienced a presence in your room (seen or heard) that scared you?

2. Do you struggle with bad thoughts about God?

3. Is it mentally hard for you to pray and read your Bible?

4. Have you heard "voices" in your head, like there was a subconscious self talking to you, or have you struggled with really bad thoughts?

5. Have you frequently had thoughts of suicide?

6. Have you ever had impulsive thoughts to kill someone, like, "Grab that knife and kill that person"?

7. Have you ever thought that you were different than others (it works for others but not for you)?

8. Do you like yourself?

9. Have you ever been involved with:
   • astral projection?
   • table lifting?
   • fortune-telling?
   • astrology?
   • Dungeons and Dragons?
   • crystals or pyramids?
   • Ouija boards?
   • automatic writing?
   • tarot cards?
   • palm reading?
   • spirit guides?
   • blood pacts?

Now compare your answers with the results of our survey:

	Percentage who answered "yes"	
	Junior high	Senior high
1. Have you ever experienced a presence in your room (seen or heard) that scared you?	50%	47%
2. Do you struggle with bad thoughts about God?	44%	54%
3. Is it mentally hard for you to pray and read your Bible?	25%	37%
4. Have you heard "voices" in your head, like there was a subconscious self talking to you, or have you struggled with really bad thoughts?	57%	70%
5. Have you frequently had thoughts of suicide?	12%	20%
6. Have you ever had impulsive thoughts to kill someone, like, "Grab that knife and kill that person"?	21%	24%
7. Have you ever thought that you were different than others (it works for others but not for you)?	73%	71%
8. Do you like yourself?	89%	32%
9. Have you ever been involved with:		
• astral projection?	2%	2%
• table lifting?	8%	8%
• fortune-telling?	8%	10%
• astrology?	11%	20%
• Dungeons and Dragons?	18%	16%

	Junior high	Senior high
• crystals or pyramids?	5%	3%
• Ouija boards?	15%	26%
• automatic writing?	1%	2%
• tarot cards?	3%	6%
• palm reading?	7%	12%
• spirit guides?	1%	2%
• blood pacts?	3%	6%

How did your responses compare to the rest? Did you notice how many things are closely tied with the mind? How well is Satan doing in the battle for your mind? Based on the results of our survey and other research I've seen, the devil appears to be winning the war for the mind of the American teenager (and adults, for that matter!).

But you can change this in your life! Daily choose the truth over the enemy's lies. Be aware that Satan can use not only occultic practices to gain a foothold to oppress and seduce us, but there are also ways that don't appear to be evil that gain him access to our minds.

How Satan Gets a Foothold

I remember the first time I went rock climbing—I thought I was going to die! My first mistake was to go with some guys who were like spiders in their ability to climb the rock faces. My second mistake was not recognizing my own limitations. My strength gave out halfway up the rock, and it became increasingly difficult to keep going. The hardest part for me was to find cracks, crevasses, and little ledges where I could get a foothold or some kind of finger hold. Without them, I wouldn't have been able to move further up.

The devil is looking for some little ledge, crack, or

crevasse he can use to infiltrate our thinking. Some of these footholds are rather blatant while others are very subtle.

Before we start looking at some of the things Satan can use as a foothold, I want to make something clear. This part of the chapter is not meant to be some sort of list of what you should and should not be doing, watching, reading, or involved in. Rather, I want you to *think* about what you're putting into your mind, and how it could be influencing not just your thinking but your life as well.

One more thing. Just because you don't find something on this list doesn't mean that you shouldn't carefully examine your participation in light of what the Bible teaches. Now let me challenge your thinking!

Party and Board Games

Bloody Mary is a popular party game among some groups of kids. A common version of the game requires someone to go into a completely darkened bathroom alone, spin around six times, face the mirror, and call upon Bloody Mary to show herself—which she often does. Other versions are just as inviting to demonic powers. It's amazing how many students see this as some kind of cute trick, not realizing that this casual exposure to the occult is a very dangerous first step into the world of darkness.

Dungeons and Dragons is by far the most popular of the fantasy role-playing games. The objectives of the game utilize sorcery and witchcraft. A practicing witch considered the game such a good tool for instructing people in paganism that he wrote a special manual showing players how to move from the game to real sorcery. We'll be discussing D&D in more detail in Part 2.

Ouija boards (the name is a combination of the French and German words for *yes*) have been around in various forms for hundreds of years. The modern version by Parker Brothers is a game board with the numbers zero through nine, the alphabet, and the words *good, bye, yes,* and *no* printed on the surface. A teardrop-shaped pointer is placed on the board.

Two players face each other over the board with their fingers lightly resting on the pointer, allowing it to move freely. The players ask questions relating to things like career, marriage, and health, and wait for the pointer to spell out answers. The game has also been used for contacting the dead and the spirit realm, developing psychic powers, and finding lost things. It's a mystery how or why the game works, even to the manufacturer. I'm sure some of it is due to muscle twitching, but you can't deny that demonic powers are involved.

Most who play with this seemingly innocent game have no idea what they are dealing with. Satanists have been known to crash Ouija board parties to help players learn how to really use the game. The Ouija board is clearly a form of divination (fortune-telling and guidance) that is forbidden by the Bible.

Crystals or pyramids. Crystals are mystical symbols of the spirit because they are solid and tangible while being transparent. Among many shaman groups, natural crystals are power objects. The word *pyramid* means "glorious light," from the Greek word *pyros* for "fire." Crystals and pyramids are most often associated with the New Age movement.

Automatic writing is practiced by spiritual mediums. The medium enters a trance and writes down the impressions that come to mind. It is an obvious counterfeit of the prophetic voice of God. God works through the active minds of His people, but occultic practices require a passive state of mind. The occult actually bypasses the mind and the personality of the person involved, and a different personality emerges.

Tarot cards come in a pack of 78 and are often regarded as the ancestor of modern playing cards. The cards are divided into the Major Arcana (22 cards) and the Minor Arcana (56). The latter consists of four suits—wands, swords, cups, and pentacles. Tarot cards are commonly used for divination.

Palm reading or palmistry is the study and interpretation of the palm of the hand for the purpose of divination. Distinguishing features of the palm include line patterns and the color and texture of the skin. People have their palms read because they want insight into the future. Isaiah 8:19,20 says that we should consult God regarding such matters.

Spirit guides are nothing more than demonic voices. New Age conferences have meditative practices that enable people to acquire their own spirit guides. Some spirits come by the laying on of hands, others through guided imagery or a mediumistic trance.

Blood pacts are an obvious counterfeit to Christianity. The shed blood of Jesus is the only basis for Christian fellowship and heritage. Satanists commonly draw blood and drink it at their ceremonies. Any blood pact is a counterfeit of Christ's work on the cross.

We have only just scratched the surface in examining party and board games with satanic and occultic connections. There is a long list of occult-oriented games, including Nightmare on Elm Street, I Ching, Tea Leaves, Tunnels and Trolls, Chivalry and Sorcery, Runne Quest, Swordbearers, and Arduin Grimore. And I have no idea what other kinds of harmful games will be introduced in the future. Guard yourself against a diversion that appears to be fun but which, in reality, may be the first step into the enemy's camp. Consider the advice in Deuteronomy 18:10-13:

Let no one be found among you who sacrifices his son or daughter in the fire, who practices divination or sorcery, interprets omens, engages in witchcraft, or casts spells, or who is a medium or a spiritist or who consults the dead. Anyone who does these things is detestable to the LORD and because of these detestable practices the LORD your God will drive out those nations before you. You must be blameless before the LORD your God.

Computer and Video Games

Electronic game manufacturers are making billions of dollars from computer and video games. While not all electronic games are evil, some can subtly lure us into the kingdom of darkness. Here are a few examples of games that dabble in occultic themes and what the manufacturers say about them.

Hero's Quest I: "Create your own character from the ground up and venture forth into a world of magic. Become a mysterious magician, a fierce fighter, or a wily thief."

Hero's Quest III: "Can you escape the bondage of the evil wizard Mannanan? . . . Learn to use magic . . . but don't get caught. . . . Find the amazing truth to your real identity."

Phantasie: "When sorcery ruled and trolls still walked the earth."

Phantasie III: The Wrath of Nikademus: "This game boasts many new features including more potent spells, weapons, and character skills."

Wizard's Crown: "Guide your valiant band through detailed tactical battles with magic and mystery."

The Secret of the Silver Blade and *Dragon Strike:* Even Dungeons and Dragons has capitalized on the popularity of computer games with these two advanced versions.

Be careful of games like these. They are more than just entertainment. Through them, Satan can be given an opportunity to infiltrate your thoughts.

Books

Seventeen-year-old Eric told me that he liked books better than videos or movies to feed his hunger for violence and the occult. He could create more graphic pictures in his mind through what he read than he could find on the screen. Considering some of the things on the bookshelf, Eric wouldn't have to work very hard to feed his hunger. Here are two examples.

Interview with a Vampire by Anne Rice. A gothic horror novel about a Louisiana landowner's toothy transformation into a vampire with a major appetite for blood. The book became a film with a hefty cast of well-known stars.

Needful Things by Stephen King. This plot follows the author's somewhat predictable pattern for wickedness. A stranger appears in a small town, plays upon the many thwarted hopes of the locals, and one by one, offers them a deal: their dreams fulfilled in exchange for their souls. The stranger? None other than Satan himself! This book also found its way to the screen as a major motion picture.

You don't have to look very far to find a considerable number of books with satanic orientation, including a series based on the game Dungeons and Dragons. Reading is a great thing to expand your mind. Just use discretion when choosing a book.

Movies and Videos

If you're like me, you enjoy going to the movies or renting videos. Again, we just need to show some discretion about what we watch. Whether it's a "Slasher" flick or something a little less gory, many films have the potential to desensitize us to evil. A steady diet of the following kinds of movies can make you a much easier target for Satan.

Army of Darkness. This is the final installment in the Evil Dead trilogy. Its department store clerk hero is time-warped into the Middle Ages where he has to fight off platoons of skeletons, zombies, and tiny ticked-off versions of himself.

Jason Goes to Hell: The Final Friday. Though this film tried to vary the formula of the typical *Friday the 13th* sex and slash, the ninth installment of impalements and dismemberments looked pretty much the same.

Body Snatchers. A teenage rebel wakes up in her new Army-base housing to find icky tendrils wrapping around her body. She realizes that alien pods are systematically replacing the humans around her. This version of the body-snatcher theme got inspiration from the films made in 1956 and 1978.

Addams Family Values. The follow-up to the 1991 hit opens with the birth of a new addition to the infamous clan—Pubert, a mustachioed baby boy. The studio spent a lot of money and time to make things more decrepit, including the backyard graveyard. The plot also contains a murderous nanny and a ghoulish groom. Not too many positive family values from this film!

Nightmare Before Christmas. This film is based on a poem about a skeleton who impersonates Santa Claus. Utilizing stop-motion puppets and animation, the director created wicked and weird characters like Oogie Boogie, a big mean burlap sack of spiders and snakes, Lock the witch, Shock the ghoul, and Barrel—a devil-like character. Tim Burton, who developed the film's creepy themes, said "If we can disturb just one child, it will have been worth it."[4]

But a movie does not have to have an occultic theme to be dangerous to our mind. Because Satan masquerades as an "angel of light" (2 Corinthians 11:14), he "candy coats" his lie to make it more appealing. For example, the comedy *Heart and Souls* is the story of an uptight yuppie who is possessed by the souls of dead people. While the film may be funny, it needs to be viewed in light of God's truth. Whether the movie is action, romance, fantasy, comedy, or adventure, watch out for subject matter dealing with sex, drugs, violence, and rebellion. God wants us to fill our minds with things that are true, pure, and proper (see Philippians 4:8).

I'm not saying that all movies and videos are bad, but you do need to be selective.

Television

Television has become not only the number-one source of information for most people today, but also the number-one value-shaper in our country. Watching TV is practically a universal activity among teenagers today. Studies indicate that the average student will have watched 17,000 hours of television and seen 18,000 simulated murders before graduating from high school.

Television broadcasts a variety of programs with connections to the occult. Sorcery, spells, power beams, incantations, ESP, crystal powers, and telepathy can be found in such Saturday morning cartoons as "X-Men," "Duckula," "The Mighty Morphin Power Rangers," "Beetlejuice," "He Man/She Ra," "Crash Dummies," and "Teenage Mutant Ninja Turtles."

In the last few years, the number of weekly prime-time shows and made-for-TV movies portraying occultic themes has increased. For example, "Quantum Leap" pictured the exploits of a time-traveler inhabiting the lives of different men and women in order to change their personal histories. The pseudo-hero is accompanied by a "guide." "Twin Peaks" was a popular show featuring an odd mixture of sex, murder, perversion, and occultism. The show's hero received midnight visits from a king-sized spirit. Other characters were possessed by demented personalities and suicidal thoughts.

Then there are the shows like "Kung Fu: The Legend Continues" or "Tales from the Crypt" that delve into the occult on a regular basis. Add to this shows like "Picket Fences," certain made-for-TV movies, and cable shows that take that occasional trip into the world of darkness, and you can definitely see the influence of evil in television.

There has also been a marked increase in the number of shows on prime time with sexual overtones—everything from "Sisters" to "Beverly Hills 90210," "Melrose Place," to "NYPD Blue." And don't forget the talk shows, the soap operas, and music videos.

Next time you turn on the TV, take a moment to think about what you'll be watching.

Music

In a national survey of teenagers, 80 percent said that music is "important" in their life.[5] Music has incredible influence, devouring large amounts of time, money, and the mind.

The roots of occultic themes in contemporary music can be traced to some of rock's earliest stars. The Rolling Stones recorded songs like "Sympathy for the Devil," "Their Satanic Majesty's Request," and "Goat's Head Soup" (a severed goat's head is used in satanic worship). Former Black Sabbath lead singer Ozzy Osbourne sang openly of demons in "Devil's Daughter."

The lyrics of current heavy metal and black metal bands are even more perverse and satanic, dealing with such topics as the death of God, sitting at Satan's left hand, sex with corpses, calling Jesus the deceiver, human sacrifice, and glorifying the names of Satan. And the lyrics are getting through. An Arkansas teenager attempted to kill his parents with a club and a butcher knife under the inspiration of a song by the metal band Slayer. He said he consulted a Ouija board and heard voices telling him to murder his parents. Police found his cassette player cued to a Slayer song titled "Altar of Sacrifice."

In the next chapter we will take more time to discuss the importance of being discerning in the music we listen to.

Drugs and Alcohol

Drug and alcohol abuse has reached epidemic proportions in our society, especially among students. Why? Partly because drugs and alcohol make you feel good. They dull the pain and the pressure of life. Partly because drugs and alcohol can give a false sense of security. They are often more reliable than family or friends. They are there when you need them, and they work every time.

It's no coincidence that the rise in occultic activity among students parallels the rise in substance abuse. There is a definite link between the two (although not everyone using drugs is involved in the occult).

Satan's goal is to capture your mind, and substances that alter your mind leave you vulnerable to his control. A 15-year-old girl summed it up this way: "Taking drugs is like getting into a strange car with a strange person and not knowing where you are going."

School

Believe it or not, another opportunity for the devil to gain a foothold in your mind is in the classroom. On a lot of campuses one of the big things being pushed today is "values clarification." It's just a nice way of saying there's no such thing as absolute truth. For example, that means there are no such things as moral absolutes regarding sex before marriage, alternative lifestyles, and honesty. It means you can believe and do whatever you want, because it's your truth—no matter how it may affect someone else.

If absolute truth does not exist, then we don't have to obey traffic laws anymore, if we decide it's not *our* truth. Instead of purchasing things in the store, you can decide to just take them, if paying for something isn't part of *your* truth. This sounds ridiculous, but that's essentially what's being taught in some classrooms. (We'll talk more about this in the chapter on the New Age in Part 2.) Remember, if Satan can get you to believe a lie, even in the classroom, then he can get you to live it.

Fashions

For many students, clothing, makeup, and hairstyle are an outward sign of an inward struggle for acceptance and identity. And some of today's fashions seem to encourage a step into the darkness to meet those needs.

In a Southern California mall not far from my office is a trendy store geared for teenagers. More than 95 percent of the items in the store are adorned with satanic and occultic symbols (see the Appendix for a list of these symbols). They are embroidered on belts, scarves, carved in jewelry, on T-shirts, ties, pants, hats, and even socks. Beware of two dangers involved in wearing clothes and other fashion articles with satanic and occultic symbols. First, the symbols represent values and a lifestyle that are contrary to the things of God. Second, as you search for ways to deal with the issues you face in day-to-day living, the devil can entice you to experiment with these symbols to see if they really have any power. Sometimes you may get more than you bargain for!

Anger and Unforgiveness

Maybe you don't really struggle with the temptation to play around with chemicals or occultic practices. And maybe you have a pretty good handle on what God would be pleased with in the area of entertainment and fashions. But the devil still has some other ways to gain a foothold in your life and infiltrate your thinking.

One of those is anger. There are times when it is okay to be angry, as long as that anger does not turn into sin (Ephesians 4:26). We should be angry about the evil, the injustice, and the immorality in the world. The Bible says that even Jesus got angry (see Matthew 21:12 and John 2:15). But anger that is selfish, vindictive, bitter, resentful, and uncontrolled can give Satan the opportunity to work his way into our mind to manipulate and control us, ultimately allowing us to be consumed by our feelings of anger.

There is another way that is closely tied to anger which can give the enemy a foothold—unforgiveness. This is Satan's greatest avenue of access to all Christians—young and old. Paul urges us to forgive one another "in order that Satan might not outwit us. For we are not unaware of his schemes" (2 Corinthians 2:10,11). Even if you have no other link to the occult in your life, an attitude of unforgiveness can turn into bitterness, becoming like a cancer to your spirit, making you an easy target for Satan's influence.

Dabbling Can Be Dangerous

I'm going to conclude this chapter by telling you a tragic story, a story that shows how dabbling can be dangerous. We must never underestimate the cunning skill of the enemy and how subtly he can lead us down the wrong path. Sometimes it does start with a game, a book, a drug. And once

Satan is given an opening, there is really no telling how things will end up.

Jim Hardy, a high school student from Missouri, came from a rotten home situation. He wanted security, acceptance, identity, and especially power to change his life. He started dabbling a little bit in the occult with things like Dungeons and Dragons and Ouija boards. He also experimented with drugs. In the process he found himself connecting with a new power—the devil.

Two of his friends got involved with him, and they all continued to experiment even more with the power of darkness. In the small town where they lived, one thing led to another, and they found themselves getting stoned and sacrificing animals to Satan on a frequent basis.

As they fed their minds on a variety of extremely violent and occultic movies and books, they started hearing voices. The drug abuse moved from marijuana to cocaine to heroin. People on campus were afraid of them because of their power and some of the things they were involved in.

Finally the voices in their heads said, "It is time. Grab a knife and kill someone." Then the voices told them that their classmate Steven Newberry was the "one." Steven was 19 and still a junior in high school because he was a little slow mentally. The plan was to lure Steven into their group with drugs and then kill him. Because Steven wanted to be accepted like everybody else, he started blowing dope with them.

They invited Steven to join them in sacrificing some small animals. Steven agreed, and they all drove out to the woods and got stoned. Jim and his two friends then told Steven to lead them down a trail to look for animals to sacrifice. Within a few minutes Jim and his friends heard the voices say, "Now. Do it now. Kill him now." So they took the baseball bats they had been carrying and beat Steven Newberry to death. They threw his lifeless body down an old abandoned well.

After they were caught, the police asked the boys why they did such a horrible thing. Their cold-blooded response was, "We did it for our Lord and Master, Satan."

This story is shocking—and sad. And what's alarming is that Jim's involvement in the occult started out as mere "dabbling," like so many students are doing today. You may be thinking that there's no way *you* would ever murder someone. But I don't think Jim or his two friends thought their experimenting with the darkness would ever lead them to take someone else's life, either.

If you or someone you know is struggling with questions about a certain activity, go to parents, a youth group leader, or a trusted friend for advice. Don't try to wrestle through it alone. Get help before things get out of control.

We've covered a lot of ground in this chapter. Everything from truth confrontations to footholds that Satan will try to use. I hope what we have discussed has caused you to think about what you are putting into your mind and about the possible consequences. Remember, not everything targeted toward you is good for you.

Learn to be more discerning and selective about what goes in, based on the truth of God's Word. As Paul wrote in Ephesians 4:27, "Do not give the devil a foothold," especially in your mind. The battle to influence and control our thinking is real, but victory is ours when we choose God's truth over Satan's lie.

Something to Think About

1. What lies has Satan been trying to infiltrate your mind with? What does the Bible specifically say about these things?

After consulting God's Word about each lie, make a two-column list on a piece of paper, one side with the lie and the other with God's truth. Take time to read and think about each one. Then commit all of this to the Lord in prayer. Specifically ask God to help you live the truth.

2. Take a few minutes to make a list of your favorite movies and TV shows. Now compare their themes with what the Bible says in Philippians 4:8. How do they measure up?

   If you find out that God would not be pleased with some of the things you have been watching, think about what else you could do with your time to feed your mind on more positive things.

3. Are you angry or bitter toward someone? What were the circumstances that caused these feelings? Spend some time in prayer, asking God to help you have a better attitude about each situation by forgiving that person and to help you move ahead in your life.

   As you work through the things we have discussed in this chapter, don't hesitate to ask a trusted friend to pray along with you and to keep you accountable for the changes you need to make.

So far in this book we've been talking about who Satan is, what he does, and the kind of battle we're in. And it's important to understand that stuff so you'll know what you're up against. In the next part we'll be talking about several specific ways Satan can influence you—sometimes without you knowing it. He has a plan to sidetrack students through subtle (and sometimes not so subtle) means. Once we understand these strategies of Satan, we can learn to take control.

PART TWO

Ways Satan Can Get to You

5

Is Rock Music
Really Satanic?

I spent a number of years as a professional musician. In seventh grade I bought my first drum set with money I had saved from a paper route. I started playing in a band that same year for parties and school dances. By the time I was in high school I was playing professionally. Eventually I ended up playing in some of the top night clubs on the West Coast, doing some studio work, and teaching others how to play drums in a music store. I even had an offer to play percussion in Elvis Presley's band.

As you might have guessed, I really love music. While recording and working in night clubs, I had the opportunity to play a lot of different styles of music. Over the years I have acquired a large collection of tapes and CDs I enjoy listening to. And I still play my drums at our evangelistic campaigns and for a public school assembly we do in cities all over the world.

So relax. I'm not out to attack your favorite groups or get you to attend a CD-smashing party. But what I *do* want you to do is carefully think about the music you listen to and the possible effect it is having on your attitudes and actions.

In this chapter we will take a look at some of the issues often related to music. We'll also see how Satan is using false teaching through and about music to misguide us, and how to establish standards for what we should and should not listen to.

Music is one of the most powerful influences in our lives today. Everywhere we go and in just about everything we do, we are surrounded by music. Not only do we listen to it on Walkmans, boom boxes, and in our cars, but it's in the stores where we shop and in the movies we watch as well. Can you imagine how dull an adventure film would be without the musical background to add excitement? Where would the heroes be without their theme songs?

Studies have revealed that the average student listens to more than 10,000 hours of music between the seventh and twelfth grades—and that doesn't include watching thousands of hours of MTV! Anything that we are exposed to this much has to have an influence on us.

Eighteen-year-old Todd says that music is the most important thing in his life: "The tapes, concerts, lights—the whole atmosphere—it's my salvation. If things bother me, I'll go into my room and lock the door, turn on the stereo and escape into my own world. I can just space. Music is a lot cheaper than drugs, and it's legal. Sometimes I'll smoke a little pot and space for a couple of hours—which is cool—but I don't need the pot. I'm a music freak! It's the place I'm the happiest. So why not indulge my music habit, even though it takes most of my cash? It's better than a drug habit or some other form of meaningless entertainment."

We identify with music, and it helps to give expression to our feelings, problems, joys, and values. Music reflects our culture and directs it as well. Music often tells the story of our times, highlighting the struggles and issues facing our society like abortion, racial tension, and AIDS. Music also directs what we do by influencing the way we style our hair, the clothes we wear, even the way we talk. Singers, songwriters, and bands often set the pace for a variety of trends that influence the way we think and what we do. In a way, you could say that musicians are preachers trying to communicate a message to us about life.

The Real Issue

The real issue we need to deal with is not the style of music we should or should not listen to, but rather we need to be concerned about the lyrics. You can find negative messages in a lot of styles of music, including country, hip-hop, punk, fusion, blues, funk, reggae, rap, metal, rave, pop, alternative, and rock music. Even the most mellow of adult easy listening can have immoral or empty lyrics. Sometimes the truth is twisted so subtly that unless you pay close attention to the lyrical content, you can be easily deceived. We need to carefully examine the philosophies songs are promoting. Colossians 2:8 says, "Don't let others spoil your faith and joy with their philosophies, their wrong and shallow answers built on men's thoughts and ideas, instead of on what Christ has said" (TLB).

Not all secular music is satanic and not all Christian music is good. Sometimes artists are singing about God, under a Christian label, and their lyrics are not accurate to what the Bible teaches or their personal lives are a disaster. Other times a person who doesn't know the Lord is singing about life in such a way that gets us to think, yet doesn't contradict what the Bible says.

Evaluate music on the timeless principles found in God's Word. First Thessalonians 5:21 says to "test everything." The apostle Paul is encouraging us to test everything—including music—against the truth of God's Word. Just because an artist or a group is not displaying occultic symbols on their albums does not mean that the content of their songs is something God would want us to feed our minds on.

So much secular music discusses all the problems in the world today but never offers any solutions. There seems to be a core message of hopelessness and a lack of solid answers. If we listen to these messages long enough, we will start to believe them. And when you lose your hope, you'll do just about anything.

There are also prominent themes of sex, violence, rebellion, suicide, and the occult in secular music. To see the effect these messages are having, all you have to do is pick up a magazine or watch the news. While music can't make you do something, it can become your philosophy. And that philosophy eventually shapes your behavior. A 19-year-old girl in Florida, who shot and killed a German tourist, said her "inspiration to murder came from a rap song." Music is not the only thing causing these problems, but it is certainly one of the most prominent contributing factors.

The New Age movement is also having an influence on some of our music today. Satan's old lie has been repackaged for the nineties with the sweeping yet subtle "Aquarian Age" philosophies. This occultic teaching is showing up on everyone's CDs from Michael Jackson to Garth Brooks.

One of country music's biggest stars, Brooks took an interesting stand on family values on one of his albums. According to Brooks, "Traditional family values encourage children to be the best they can be. If your parents are black and white, if your parents are the same sex, that's still traditional family values to me."[1]

This was his way of explaining the song "We Shall Be Free," which leads off his album "The Chase," and includes his vote of support for same-sex couples. "When we're free to love anyone we choose," he sings, "then we shall be free."[2]

Brooks who always puts himself forward as a very religious performer now has to walk a tightrope. "It's tough for me, because I love the Bible," he explains. "For those people that feel religiously that homosexuality is wrong, are they not as right as the people who feel homosexuality is right?"[3]

Did you catch Garth's underlying philosophy about life? *Relative truth.* He even went so far as to say that the Bible is all relative, depending on what you believe. Not only is this a New Age teaching (which we will look at more closely in chapter 8), but it's a philosophy straight from the lips of the enemy.

In no way am I saying that Garth Brooks is a Satan worshiper, but do you see how subtly the devil is using his music to promote his occultic lies? This is a great example to remind us that we need to test everything we listen to against the truth of God's Word, no matter what the style of music.

Satan will do everything he can to pervert and dilute God's truth, especially in such a powerful medium as music. Be careful not to get misled by some rock star wearing a cross, dedicating an album to God, praying before a concert, or thanking Him for an award. I distinctly remember signing autographs before I was a Christian with "God Bless You," only because it looked good. I had no clue at that time what it meant or who God really was. Sometimes something will sound Christian when it's really not—for example, "Pray" by M.C. Hammer, "Like a Prayer" by Madonna, "Can't Find My Way Home" by the House of Lords, or music by the Irish rock band U2.

We need to discern whether someone's lifestyle really matches what they are saying. We also need to find out if they are talking about the god of this world or the God of the Bible.

Don't be too quick to call someone a Christian just because they are dedicating an album to God or using some Christian buzzword. Check to see if their talk matches their walk. In the book of Ephesians, the apostle Paul talks about the lifestyle of one who is a true follower of Christ. In 4:1 he writes, "As a prisoner of the Lord, then, I urge you to live a life worthy of the calling you have received." Then in 5:8 he says, "For you were once darkness, but now you are light in the Lord. Live as children of light." In other words, to claim the name of Christ means there must have been a change that took place in your life. You can't talk about God for five minutes at a concert and then mock Him the other 23 hours and 55 minutes of the day. Carefully examine, in light of the Bible, the message this artist is presenting.

Satan loves to confuse and frustrate us. He enjoys mixed messages, like an ungodly musician wearing a cross, and half-truths, like a group who claims to worship Satan just so they can sell a CD or a Christian group singing unbiblical lyrics. I believe he wields a lot of power in the area of music, so let's take a moment to talk about what Satan can and cannot do in regard to the music you're listening to.

How Satan Can (and Cannot) Use Music

Slayer was just a Los Angeles garage band who wanted to make it big. They went to a management company who advised them to act like they worshiped Satan—it would help them go straight to the top. That's just what they did, and they were a major influence on the heavy metal scene for a long period of time. When questioned about their worship of the devil, the group denied their involvement with the enemy and said they were simply into sex, drugs, and rock 'n' roll. Yet to many of their fans, devil worship looked like the cool thing to do because of the band members' behavior.

Only God truly knows their heart, but it's pretty obvious by their lyrics and lifestyle that Slayer's message is contrary to what the Bible teaches. In Matthew 12:34 we read, "For out of the overflow of the heart the mouth speaks."

There are a lot of groups who are into Satan, use occultic symbols, and write songs that glorify the devil. Because of society's hero worship of musicians, these people are being used to lead their followers down a path to hell. And even those who just play the game so they can sell CDs or just lead ungodly lives are pawns in the hands of the enemy to deceive, confuse, frustrate, and mislead. Proverbs 19:27 says, "Stop listening to teaching that contradicts what you know is right" (TLB). The only way to know what is right is to know God's Word.

Along with Satan's influence comes a lot of confusion about his role in rock music. For example, I hear well-meaning people talk about the syncopated satanic beat found in popular music. Yet there is absolutely nothing to support this concept. Think about it. Our world is filled with syncopated rhythm. Listen to an animal running or a flat tire thumping down the road. Put your hand over your heart—that's rhythm! We are dealing with an issue of taste when it comes to the beat of music. Beats aren't satanic. We should be concerned with the lyrical content and the lifestyle of the musicians.

There is also nothing that makes the beat of rock music any more erotic than any other style. Any type of music can feed your hormones, if that's where your mind is focused. Elevator music can be sensual, depending on what your brain has been fed. We are dealing with a spiritual battle for the *mind.* Jesus said, "The good man brings good things out of the good stored up in his heart, and the evil man brings evil things out of the evil stored up in his heart. For out of the overflow of his heart his mouth speaks" (Luke 6:45). If your heart is storing up sexy images from music videos or sensual lyrics from the latest hit, music is going to be erotic for you—no matter the beat.

Music TV and Comics

Since 1981 an entire generation has been growing up on MTV and music videos. According to Brandon Tartikoff, former president of NBC Entertainment, "MTV is an institution. There is a whole generation out there molded and influenced by it."[4] The two incredibly powerful tools of music and television come together in MTV. The music hooks us and the visual reinforces the message of the lyrics in our mind.

There is something else connected with the music industry that has become a powerful tool in the hands of the devil—music comics. A good friend of mine sent me a copy of an issue that his son, a freshman in high school, brought home one day. This particular series by Metal Thunder Comics is called *Rock Fantasies.* The series has issues featuring Pink Floyd, Led Zepplin, Guns N' Roses, The Rolling Stones, KISS, Jimi Hendrix, Def Leppard, David Bowie, The Doors, Rock Vixens, Sex Pistols, and Van Halen.

The issue my friend sent me was titled "Metallica in Step Dude and Battle of Hallowed Ground."[5] The host of the comic is named Crypt Keeper Cliff and he "unfolds tales of a more sinister nature." In the story called "Step Dude," the lyrics of a Metallica song help three brothers get revenge on their new stepfather. Using the lyrics from the song "The Thing That Should Not Be," off the album "Masters of Puppets," the three teenagers contact Ghorhasthor, the dark demon of revenge. Before the demon grants their request, he requires a sacrifice. So after beheading the maid, Ghorhasthor promptly closes in on his next prey—the new stepfather. The rest of the comic is filled with more of the same.

It doesn't take a rocket scientist to realize that comics like this are another subtle way the devil can infiltrate our imagination with evil.

These are just some of the ways the enemy attempts to confuse and frustrate us with false teaching related to music. There is no way in a book like this I could mention all the various bands and singers who are in some way linked to the occult or sing "worldly philosophies." Instead, I gave you some general ideas of what is out there, knowing that new styles and groups appear on the scene every month. Once again, the objective has been to get you to think about what you are putting into your mind.

How Does Your Music Measure Up?

In order to effectively deal with the impact music is having in our lives, we must develop a biblically based strategy for evaluating the music we listen to, so we can make selective and better choices. Keep in mind this simple principle: "Garbage in, garbage out." Here are some ideas to get you started.

1. How many hours per day do you spend each day listening to music? watching MTV? watching other TV shows?

2. How much time do you spend reading and studying the Bible each day?

3. Based on your answers to questions 1 and 2, who or what is having the greater influence on your thought life?

4. What does the music you listen to cause you to feel emotionally? What does it cause you to think about? Why do you listen to the groups and singers that you do?

5. List your favorite styles of music, then under each style list the themes or subjects that each presents

(for example: sex, rebellion, suicide, love, etc.). What does the Bible say about each one of these? (If you're not sure, look up each word in a concordance for some specific verses.)

6. Have you ever done something based on what you have listened to or watched on TV? Be specific (language, hairstyle, clothes, etc.).

7. Ask yourself, "Is what the songwriter wants me to believe or do right for me as a Christian?" Use Philippians 4:8 (CEV) as a standard for evaluation:

> "Finally, my friends, keep your minds on
>> whatever is *true,*
>> whatever is *pure,*
>> whatever is *right,*
>> whatever is *holy,*
>> whatever is *friendly,*
>> whatever is *proper.*
>
> Don't ever stop thinking about what is *truly worthwhile and worthy of praise.*"

Compare song lyrics to this verse and see how they measure up.

It's important not just to be a sponge and soak everything up. Be selective in the music you listen to. Keep thinking about the music you listen to. Don't give Satan an avenue into your mind with the tunes of today. Keep sifting and evaluating, using the Bible as your standard. It may be hard to stop listening to a favorite band, but God will honor your desire to please Him and be obedient.

And if you haven't done so already, why not check out some contemporary Christian music? You'll probably be able to find your favorite style of music with positive lyrics. That can really encourage you in your walk with Christ.

Something to Think About

1. What are some of the dangers of being a sponge—just soaking up every message of the songs you listen to? Be specific.

2. Name one secular rock song you think that a Christian could learn a lot from. Why did you pick that particular song?

3. Suppose you were a parent. What would you tell your kids about listening to music?

6

A Game Turns Deadly

Three teenagers influenced by the fantasy role-playing game Dungeons and Dragons made a pact to remain friends—even when it came to the coldly calculated slaying of one of their own families.

Billy Smith, 18, Joel Henry, 19, and Scott Kammeyer, 19, had been friends for years and were heavily involved in D&D. Henry was the "master strategist" while Smith and Kammeyer were the "PC's" or "play characters." By the rules of the game the players are to be completely obedient to the "master strategist."

When Henry faced relocation to Texas, he and his friends devised a plan to maintain their friendship. They decided to kill the Kammeyer family because Scott's parents had a vehicle, some weapons inside the house, and some money—at least more than anyone else. (They got $185.)

They ambushed Scott's parents after luring them home from work with a concocted report of a problem with the toilet in the master bedroom. During the slaying, "master strategist" Henry, who stands 5 feet, 2 inches tall and weighs 105 pounds, waited outside and listened for gunshots fired by "play character" Smith, who is 6 feet, 8 inches tall and weighs 340 pounds.

The bodies of Scott's parents and brother were found on a Saturday evening in their home on Gibson Street in Bakersfield, California. The murder weapons—a knife and a shotgun—were destroyed and thrown into a ditch in Mexico by the three, who were on their way to South America.[1]

By the time the boys had reached Mexico, though, the money was already spent. They were arrested when they crossed back into California to meet friends for more money. Each one confessed to the crime when interviewed by detectives.

Late on that Saturday night Scott Kammeyer and his two friends shed their teenage identities and became powerful warriors of destruction. When I talked with sheriff's official Glenn Johnson, he said the three lived in and out of fantasy and reality so much that they finally lost track of where they were. The crime scene was littered with a lot of D&D paraphernalia, showing a direct link between the game and the slaying.

When Billy, Scott, and Joel began playing D&D, they were no different than millions of other teenagers and adults who get hooked on this popular "mind" game. One of the attractions of the game is to be able to escape with a few friends into a fantastical setting where elves, halflings, and wizards do battle and usually win.

According to TSR Hobbies, Inc., the manufacturer, about 10 million copies of the game and its successor, Advanced Dungeons and Dragons, have been sold worldwide since 1974. But this fantasy role-playing game (FRP) has attracted controversy in just about every place it is sold.

What's Wrong with Dungeons and Dragons?

Alana Kammeyer often told friends how much she worried

about her son's addiction to the game. Apparently he was having problems in school because his only interest was in computer games like D&D.

Critics of the game say slayings like the Kammeyers' are no surprise. Dungeons and Dragons invites violence and negativism and twists the players' minds.

Since the game was invented by insurance salesman Guy Gygax, D&D has been linked to more than 50 teenage suicides, according to the National Coalition on Television Violence. The most notorious murder involving D&D was chronicled in Joe McGinniss' 1991 bestseller, *Cruel Doubt*. The book describes the 1988 murder of wealthy Leith Von Stein and the savage beating of his wife, Bonnie, in a plot created by Bonnie's son Chris and his two friends. The three concocted their plan during a D&D session and carried it out so Chris would inherit a lot of money.

Supporters of the game say it is one of the most creative on the market, encouraging skills like psychic reading and writing. Even the Association for Gifted-Creative Children endorses the game. It's said to be a thinking person's game.

I'm all for encouraging the development of creativity. In fact, I believe God is the one who gives us the ability to be creative. It's up to us to use it to glorify good or evil. It seems to me that learning psychic reading and writing is nowhere near the best use of our creative energy, nor is it something that God is pleased with. I want to encourage you to be creative, but find more positive ways to do it.

There are two main forms of playing the game: *role playing*, where participants take on the part of a character and work through a series of confrontations and mysteries; and *war games*, where battles are played out with catapults, tanks, starships, or some other weapon on a regular game board or defined playing field. The role-playing games seem to be more popular by far. Billy, Scott, and Joel lost track of what was role playing and what was real life, but they didn't start out that way. It was a very subtle transformation.

The game is available in many versions, ranging from a board game to sophisticated computer programs. And there are essentially two game "systems"—advanced and basic. A basic box set of D&D costs about $20 and includes a booklet of written adventures to follow, rules, dice, and maps. Every month TSR puts out three new adventures, but many players like to craft their own.

The main part of D&D takes place in an imaginary world of dragons and magic. Characters are good and evil with the more evil and violent ones possessing the greater life expectancy. (That should make you think twice!) Players in the game earn power based on the number of enemies and monsters they kill. "Campaigns or adventures" can take up to one year to finish playing.

TSR Hobbies, Inc. has been named in several lawsuits in the past over a teenager's involvement with the game and a related suicide or killing. In 1983 the company started inserting a warning statement in the instruction manual about players overidentifying with game characters: "The more the two [reality and fantasy] are kept apart, the better your games will be."

There are dozens more fantasy role-playing games like D&D on the market today. Go to any game store or pick up a computer software catalog and you will find many other games containing the same dark objectives. And, amazingly, they are always presented as a form of "creative entertainment for those who want to challenge their minds."

Some say that only those who are "unstable" to begin with will commit violent acts because of their involvement with a game like D&D. Others say that just because the game is played and the participant is obsessed with the game doesn't mean the game itself caused the violent act.

In research for a previous book I wrote, several thousand students were surveyed from across the country regarding their involvement with various forms of occultism, including D&D.[2] The results showed that 43 percent of the students who have played the game reported impulsive thoughts to kill, as opposed to only 16 percent among students who had not played the game. Once again we come back to the battle for the mind and the possible effects of exposure to the occult.

How closely linked is D&D to other forms of the occult? Isaac Bonewits, a practicing witch, considered it such a good tool for instructing people in paganism that he wrote a special manual showing players how to move from the game into real sorcery. For convicted teenage killer Sean Sellers, the game fueled his hunger for darkness and eventually led him into the trap of Satan worship, the occult, and murder.

The problem is that people who get involved with FRPs sometimes lose track of what is real and what is fantasy. Then they become desensitized to evil, violence, and the occult. A little bit of curiosity can lead to an unhealthy fascination and ultimately to an uncontrolled obsession.

That's not to say that everyone who plays an FRP is going to end up like Scott Kammeyer and his friends. A game by itself can't make you kill someone or commit a violent act. But by participating in these type of games, you are allowing yourself to be gradually seduced or brainwashed. Overexposure to evil characters and themes *can* corrupt your values and open your mind up to demonic powers. You may not commit a particular act because of the game, but you can become much more accepting of darkness, which could pave the way for the enemy to gain a foothold in your life and infiltrate your mind.

For many teenagers and adults alike, games like D&D are the first step into the world of the occult. Satan slowly sneaks in, attempting to distract, disillusion, and destroy.

You may never go as far as guys like Billy, Joel, and Scott, but the devil only has to keep you slightly off track to cause you to miss God's best for your life.

What the Bible Has to Say

If you're serious about your relationship with Christ and want the very best He has to offer, you need to take His Word so seriously that you will practice obeying it in every dimension of your life—including entertainment and recreation.

To help you do this, let's check out what the Bible says about some of the key elements involved in playing Dungeons and Dragons. Then make your decision about the game based on the standards of God's Word.

Evil

> Do not swerve to the right or the left; keep your foot from evil (Proverbs 4:27).

> Since these people refused even to think about God, he let their useless minds rule over them. That's why they do all sorts of indecent things. They are evil, wicked, and greedy, as well as mean in every possible way. They want what others have, and they murder, argue, cheat, and are hard to get along with. They gossip, say cruel things about others, and hate God. They are proud, conceited, and boastful, always thinking up new ways to do evil. These people don't respect their parents. They are stupid, unreliable, and don't have any love or pity for others. They know God has said that anyone who acts this way deserves to die. But they keep

on doing evil things, and they even encourage others to do them (Romans 1:28-32 CEV).

Dear friend, do not imitate what is evil but what is good. Anyone who does what is good is from God. Anyone who does what is evil has not seen God (3 John 11).

God has a plan and purpose for each one of us. He has set a path of life before us that will give us the greatest degree of happiness and satisfaction. But that means we need to stay on the path and not get sidetracked on detours, including evil in any form. God feels so strongly about the hazards of evil that He doesn't even want us to imitate it.

Magic, Spells, and Sorcery

Let no one be found among you who sacrifices his son or daughter in the fire, who practices divination or sorcery, interprets omens, engages in witchcraft, or casts spells, or who is a medium or spiritist or who consults the dead (Deuteronomy 18:10,11).

Blessed are those who wash their robes, that they may have the right to the tree of life and may go through the gates into the city. Outside are the dogs, those who practice magic arts, the sexually immoral, the murderers, the idolaters and everyone who loves and practices falsehood (Revelation 22:14,15).

The Bible leaves no room for doubt where God stands on the use of magic, spells, or sorcery in any form. God wants us to have nothing to do with them. Why? Because they are harmful to us, probably even more so when it comes to entertainment. When we are having "fun" with something, it is easy to lose sight of the dangers. Remember, God is for you and always has your best interest at heart.

Find Alternatives

Even after learning of the dangers of FRPs, some students I've talked to say they have a hard time stopping their involvement with the games. Many tell me they miss the mental stimulation and challenge. I assure them that there is nothing wrong with using your imagination, as long as what you are doing is pleasing to God.

Being a Christian doesn't mean you're brain-dead or unimaginative or that you can't have any fun. Quite the opposite is true! Get together with your friends and design a fantasy role-playing game with biblical or historical themes, using intrigue, skill, and wisdom as your weapons to outwit your opponents. (By the way, if you do develop a game, let me know so I can share the idea with others!)

The Bible says that we have the mind of Christ (1 Corinthians 2:16). Talk about creative power! We should be the most creative, on-the-edge people on the planet. We should be the ones the world tries to imitate rather than the other way around. But for that to happen, we have to let Christ control our thoughts.

Jesus said, "I came so that everyone would have life, and have it in its fullest" (John 10:10 CEV). Jesus made it possible for us to live the most exciting, fun-filled life imaginable. So start having fun—Jesus' way!

Here are a couple of ideas for alternative ways to challenge yourself mentally. First, if you're into fantasy or sci-fi novels, read books by C.S. Lewis, J.R.R. Tolkien, or Stephen Lawhead—all Christian men with brilliant minds and incredible imaginations. If you are looking for something related even more closely to spiritual warfare, read Frank Peretti's novels.

Second, look for an alternative to FRPs. Try and find games that help you to pursue and develop godly characteristics in a challenging way. A good verse to keep in mind as a guideline is Galatians 5:22:

> God's Spirit makes us loving, happy, peaceful, patient, kind, good, faithful, gentle, and self-controlled. There is no law against behaving in any of these ways (CEV).

I'll be honest with you. If you have decided to give up D&D or a similar game or activity because you realize it's not working for good in your life, it won't be easy. So don't try and do it alone. Begin by asking God in prayer for help and strength. Then go to a Christian adult you trust and tell him or her about the decision. That person can keep you accountable and be a real source of encouragement as well as answer any questions you may have.

We learned in this chapter that fantasy role-playing games not only influence our thinking, but they have the potential to cause havoc in our lives as well. It's important to guard against overexposing our minds to evil philosophies and themes.

It will be difficult letting go of something that has been consuming vast amounts of your time and energy, but it's like dealing with any other habit that needs to be broken: Take it one day at a time. Avoid putting unrealistic expectations on yourself. Be careful not to procrastinate.

All the resources of heaven are available to you to help you win in this dimension of your life. Take the first step toward change and God will help you to do the rest!

Something to Think About

1. Read James 1:8. How does this verse apply to a Christian involved with FRPs?

2. How can you tell the difference between fantasy and reality?

3. What does it mean to participate in a game (or anything else) that glorifies evil? (Start by looking up the definition of *participate*.)

4. What would be the best way to help a family member or friend who is addicted to D&D see the dangers of the game?

7

Witchcraft Isn't Cool

According to a popular magazine for girls, witchcraft is "cool." *Sassy* interviewed several witches, including a 16-year-old aspiring young actress, for their article "Witchcraft Is a Religion."[1]

Laurie Cabot, the 60-year-old official witch of Salem, Massachusetts, and one of more than nine million witches worldwide, says witchcraft is an earth-based religion with heavy environmental overtones. According to the article in *Sassy*, witches are not Satanists and don't believe in evil, Satan, or sacrificing animals. Doing evil is supposedly against one of the basic principles of their religion—if you do anything bad, it comes back to you three times. Any magic witches do is "for the good of all," as they say at the end of spells.

Witchcraft, or Wicca, has been a legally recognized religion in the United States since 1985 and has eight major holidays that revolve around the changing of the seasons. On these days, covens, which are groups of three to 13 witches, form magic circles where they perform rituals and read spells.

Also "cool," according to *Sassy*, is the fact that witchcraft has always been a very woman-centered religion. Although witches believe in many goddesses and gods, they maintain that the universe was created by a goddess because only women have the ability to create life by giving birth. Most witches are women, although more men are becoming interested in witchcraft.

Magic is a very important part of witchcraft. Any witch has the power to make things happen. According to Laurie Cabot in her book *Power of the Witch: The Earth, the Moon, and the Magical Path to Enlightenment*, magic is performed in an altered state of consciousness called *alpha*, in which fewer brain waves register per second. She gives step-by-step instructions for going into alpha by counting back from the number seven and relaxing. Apparently witches can use this altered state to do all of their magic, from something as simple as getting a parking place to work as serious as cleaning up the environment.

Cabot's book goes on to describe how anyone can learn to do these things, as well as how spells are written, how words are used to conduct energy, and how magic potions are made.

Cats are important to witches because they are their connection to the animal world. They call them *familiars*. Witches use crystals and wear pentacles—a five-pointed star inside a circle that is said to bring wisdom and protection. Witches wear black for rituals because it contains all the colors of the rainbow.

A lot of people who study witchcraft are searching for spiritual truth and the supernatural. Kaytee, a 16-year-old high school junior who wants to be an actress, is a witch. So is her mother, her father, and her eight-year-old sister. Kaytee's parents are first-degree witches, but she is still practicing for initiation. She is learning the basics of alpha and about the gods and goddesses of the magic circle. Everyone at her school knows she is into witchcraft, although most don't understand it.[2]

Kaytee says she is going to use her first spell to help her get the part of Peter Pan in the school play. "It's like prayer," she says. "I will project that I will get this part of Peter Pan in the musical, harm me none and for the good of all."

Even though for some the feminist and environmental aspects of witchcraft are enticing, the big draw is power. According to Laurie Cabot, "Witchcraft is a connectedness to everything, so you can center yourself and feel as if you can control some of your environment a little more. I think teenagers today need their own power. They need to feel that they can help shape the future."[3]

What the Bible Has to Say

As you can tell, the "Old Religion" (as it is known) of witchcraft is experiencing renewed interest today, especially among teenagers. But before you start thinking it's "cool," let's see what the Bible has to say.

Witchcraft can basically be defined as the performance of magic forbidden by God for nonbiblical ends. The word *witchcraft* is related to the old English word *wiccan*, the "practice of magical arts."

Both the Old and the New Testaments make repeated references to the practice of witchcraft and sorcery. In every instance where these practices are mentioned, they are condemned by God. The Bible condemns all forms of witchcraft, including sorcery, astrology, and magic.

God is so concerned about this subject that He very specifically warns us in His Word to stay away from it. In 2 Chronicles 33 we read about a man named Manasseh who became a king at the ripe old age of 12. He did evil in the eyes of the Lord and paid a price for his bad choices. Here's what God said about Manasseh's involvement in witchcraft:

> He [Manasseh] sacrificed his sons in the fire in
> the Valley of Ben Hinnom, practiced sorcery,
> divination and witchcraft, and consulted me-
> diums and spiritists. He did much evil in the
> eyes of the LORD, provoking him to anger
> (2 Chronicles 33:6).

Just because this story is about a king who lived a few
thousand years ago doesn't mean that God has changed His
mind about witchcraft. This warning is just as relevant to us
as it was in previous generations. Provoking God to anger is
not a very smart thing to do. Why would God get angry
about this kind of practice? Because He wants us to rely on
Him for guidance, power, and direction. He is our strength
and our life, not the forces of darkness.

In the book of Galatians, the apostle Paul warns us to
beware of the strong pull of the flesh that can cause us to fall
into sin. Let's look at Galatians 5:19-21:

> The acts of the sinful nature [flesh] are obvious:
> sexual immorality, impurity and debauchery
> [shamelessness]; idolatry and witchcraft; hatred,
> discord, jealousy, fits of rage, selfish ambition,
> dissensions, factions [cliques] and envy; drunk-
> enness, orgies, and the like. I warn you, as I did
> before, that those who live like this will not
> inherit the kingdom of God.

What an ugly list of sins witchcraft has been included
in! Carefully consider Paul's warning at the end of this
passage regarding the kingdom of God. The end of verse 21
is a reminder that if you continue to live in this kind of sin,
you are in a dangerous position. It means you are not a child
of God.

Watching Out for Witchcraft

As Christians, we need to be prepared to respond to the influence of witchcraft that we run into in our daily lives. Things associated with witchcraft can show up in a variety of ways in many different places.

Think about the movies you go to see. Not all movies are bad, but some do promote the principles of witchcraft. Take, for example, the film *Hocus Pocus*, starring Bette Midler, Sarah Jessica Parker, and Kathy Najimy. The plot portrays the three as long-dead seventeenth-century witches who are brought back to life one Halloween to suck the life out of children.[4] It's silly, scary, and magical all at the same time; but it can also confuse us as to the response God would want us to have toward witchcraft. When the film was first released it was interesting to watch a number of witches come out against the movie because it portrayed them in a negative light. I guess the truth hurts!

Satan also has a way of making witchcraft look fashionable and appealing. Stevie Nicks, the female lead singer of the now-defunct rock band Fleetwood Mac, is a self-avowed white witch.[5] Yet she and the band performed in a reunion concert at one of the parties celebrating the inauguration of President Bill Clinton. When a witch is performing at that level, it can deceive you into thinking that witchcraft can't be all that evil.

Witchcraft and its influences can also be found in games for your PC, fantasy role-playing games, board games, and even comic books. And even more popular is the influence of witchcraft in the environmental movement. There has never been a generation so environmentally conscious as today's generation. And witches are at the forefront, encouraging us to "be nice to mother earth." While we need to do our part in being environmentally sensitive, we also need to be careful not to get things out of balance.

God has called us to be caretakers of the planet. In Genesis 2:15 we read, "The Lord placed the man in the Garden of Eden as its gardener, to tend and care for it" (TLB). But the Bible also teaches us that we are to worship the Creator, not the creation. In Exodus 20:3 God says, "You may worship no other god than me" (TLB). While witchcraft may appear to be helping the environment, it goes about it in the wrong way. Remember to keep your eyes and heart centered on God as you strive to do the right thing.

Going tò the Right Source

What if a good friend starts to show an interest in magic spells? How should you respond? Start by praying and asking God to help you find out why your friend would be interested in witchcraft. Sometimes people start playing around with this stuff at parties out of curiosity. They want to see if there's really any power that can be gained. Dabbling like this can be dangerous; it can be a gateway to the occult.

For others, a fascination with witchcraft comes from a sincere search for power to change their life or to deal with the pain of a broken home, rejection, or hopelessness. While witchcraft may appear to offer immediate power for change, it is temporary at best. It also leaves God totally out of the picture and relies on power from the darkness.

The only power that we need to handle the pressures of life is found in the resurrection of Jesus Christ. The same power that God used to bring Jesus back to life after being in the grave for three days is available to help us overcome the challenges in our daily life. That's power!

The best way to apply this power is through prayer. When you or someone you care about is facing tough times, ask God for His strength and wisdom to face the situation. Put your energy and effort in prayerfully seeking God's help and answers. Also make sure you are getting a steady diet of answers from God's Word. The Bible is God's handbook for living, and it contains supernatural guidance that only God can give. (We'll talk more about this in Chapter 13, "Choose Your Weapons.")

Don't fall into the trap of quick, "microwavable" answers gained from chants and spells. Go to the author of life itself, and trust God.

Satan will do anything he can to candy coat evil, making it easier to seduce us away from our family, church, and God. Don't be confused by Laurie Cabot and other witches who sprinkle bits of truth in with the lies through witchcraft. It's okay to be concerned about the environment, equal treatment of the sexes, and other things that plague our society. Do your part in making positive changes. But always take your stand and direction based on the absolute truth of God's Word. Respond how He would have you respond to the challenges of life.

Knowing Jesus and serving Him is the ultimate "cool"!

Something to Think About

1. There are many places in the Bible where God addresses the subject of witchcraft. Check out what God says in each passage and what our response should be.

Deuteronomy	Micah 5:12
18:9-13	Nahum 3:4
2 Kings 9:22	Revelation 21:8

2. Take some time to carefully evaluate your life in light of Galatians 5:19-21. If you are caught in the trap of one or

more of the sins mentioned, let God know you're sorry. Ask Him to help you stop giving in to this temptation. You'll never be happy as long as you're being disobedient to God.

3. What is one way you can personally respond to the problems with the environment in a way that honors God? When, where, and with whom do you need to accomplish this action?

4. Do you have a friend or family member who is messing around with witchcraft? Besides praying for this person, how else does God want you to respond and help him or her?

———————

8

The New Age

If you've had enough of reality, buckle your seat belts and hang on! "Virtual reality," also called artificial or simulated reality, is headed to your house. Computer-created "VR" worlds are showing up in military simulators, game arcades, and the plots of futuristic thrillers, like Stephen King's *The Lawnmower Man*. Virtual reality has the potential of opening a Wonderland that Alice never dreamed of. You can hurtle through faraway galaxies, cycle over the Alps, or race a Ferrari at 200 mph and never leave your family room.

Virtual reality has the potential of becoming the ultimate entertainment or the ultimate drug. Some people have even called it electronic LSD. Available virtual world systems transform reality by means of wraparound goggles plugged into a computer. The computer sends images to miniature screens inside the goggles to create a 3-D, you-are-really-there effect. The scene changes as you turn your head. Point the glove "studded" with sensors that you're wearing to the left and an on-screen object, like a plane, heads left. In the other hand you may be holding additional controls. VR designers call this "human-factor engineering"—a manipulation of the senses.

At the $1.2 million BattleTech Virtual World Center in Chicago, players get a feel of war. You squeeze into a cockpit and appear on-screen as a 30-foot-long robot tank to be maneuvered against opponents in other war machines. Cost: $7 for ten minutes of heavy action. In England, $35,000 "Virtuality" games in several arcades can give you the taste of *Top Gun*-style jet piloting. Using gloves and headgear, you and an opponent dogfight to the death. And with virtual golf, theme parks, medical applications, and more being added daily, the sky is the limit to what can turn into reality.

Playing make-believe war games, driving race cars, or even joining the action in a movie theater with gloves and goggles can be challenging, fun, and entertaining. But it's not real. There are people today, however, who honestly believe they can change reality into any form they want. They believe, "Reality is what you make it," and they are part of the New Age movement.

Time magazine calls the New Age "a combination of spirituality and superstition, fad and force, about which the only thing certain is that it is not new."[1] Essentially, the New Age is nothing but ancient Hinduism and occultism repackaged. Leaders within the movement say it is amazing what you can get people to do when you take away the Hindu and the occultic terminology and use language for the nineties.

The New Age can be defined as the growing penetration of Eastern and occultic mysticism into Western culture. The term *New Age* refers to the Aquarian Age, which some New Agers believe is dawning, bringing with it an era of enlightenment, peace, prosperity, and perfection. That's exactly what Satan would like us to think! In reality, the New Age movement is simply opening the doors to his destructive influence in our culture even wider than before.

The Set Up

The New Age is another weapon in the devil's arsenal to lure us away from God's truth. The following statistics give us a brief glimpse of the progress Satan is making in shaping our thinking.

- 45 percent of all Americans believe that ghosts exist.

- 31 percent of all Americans believe that some people have magical powers.

- 34 million Americans are concerned with inner growth, including mysticism.

- 42 percent of Americans believe they have been in contact with someone who has died.

- 67 percent of Americans report having psychic experiences like extra-sensory perception (ESP).

- 30 million Americans—roughly one in four—believe in reincarnation, a key principle of New Age faith.

- 14 percent of Americans endorse the work of spirit mediums or trance channelers.

- 67 percent of Americans read astrology reports (36 percent believe they are scientific).

- A northern Illinois university survey found that more than half of Americans think extraterrestrial beings have visited earth (a belief held in many New Age circles).[2]

- 28 percent believe in witchcraft, 24 percent in black magic, and 20 percent in voodoo.[3]

It's amazing how popular the New Age has become. You can go into almost any bookstore and find a massive section of books relating to various aspects of the New Age. Entire magazines are devoted to the New Age. And New Age music continues to gain popularity with musicians like Yanni and Tangerine Dream.

New Age concepts have also been steadily introduced and made popular by a variety of celebrities. Have you seen the Psychic Network "info-mercials" hosted by the Grammy award-winning singer Dionne Warwick? For several dollars per minute you can have access to your own personal psychic to help you find answers about your future, love life, and even career choices.

Or how about New Age guru and bestselling author Anthony Robbins? He has his own "info-mercial" with a host of celebrities giving advice on how to change your life. His three-and-a-half day "Unleash the Power Within" seminar begins with "Fear into Power—The Firewalk Experience," an ancient occultic practice.

New Age and occultic themes can be found in movies and TV series like the Star Wars saga and the Star Trek series. New Age products and gadgets seem to be flooding the marketplace: singing Tibetan bowls, crystals, pyramids, tarot cards, charms, fortune-telling devices, computer software, and even "rebirthing" tanks.

The New Age movement has become more than a fad. For many, it's a lifestyle. From the outside, the New Age movement is very appealing. It's trying to accomplish some good things. New Agers want to take care of the homeless problem and eliminate all disease and racial tension in the world. And they are very concerned about the environment.

But probably the biggest appeal of the New Age is that you can be your own god. That's the same desire that got Satan kicked out of heaven in the first place (Isaiah 14:12-14).

Six Principles of New Age Thinking

The following six principles of New Age thinking form the "revolutionary understanding" shared by those involved in the movement. As you will see, each one of these principles is a clever, subtle counterfeit of biblical Christianity. (A glossary of New Age terms is found in the Appendix.)

1. All Is One. One Is All.

According to New Agers, every little particle in the universe and every piece of matter everywhere is interconnected. Everything swims in this huge cosmic interconnected ocean. There is no difference between rocks, trees, humans, animals, and God. We are all the same. The reason we have problems in our world today is not because of evil, but ignorance. We are ignorant of the fact that we are all interconnected.

The Bible teaches something entirely different:

> For by him all things were created: things in heaven and on earth, visible and invisible, whether thrones or powers or rulers or authorities; all things were created by him and for him. He is before all things, and in him all things hold together (Colossians 1:16,17).

God is *separate* from His creation. The Bible also tells us that we are separated from God because of our sin (Romans 3:23). In New Age teaching there is no need for forgiveness since we are all just one vast interconnected ocean.

2. God Is Everything. Everything Is God.

New Agers say that everything in creation is part of God—trees, snails, people, etc. Everything has a divine

(God-like) nature. It is part of God. The idea of a personal God needs to be abandoned. You don't need a savior because you are part of God. If a god (he or she) does exist at all, "it" really just started a "big bang" many years ago and is now just an impersonal force floating around in the cosmos somewhere.

What are the implications of a principle like this? It allows the Wiccan religion to worship the creation, "mother earth" (rocks, sun, moon, etc.), rather than the creator (God). New Agers say that since we are all gods, we might as well get good at it. In Genesis 3:5 Satan deceitfully tells Adam and Eve that if they eat the fruit of a particular tree they will be like God.

The New Agers have reduced God to the human level so He is no different than you and me. If God is an impersonal force, He doesn't need to be served, obeyed, or loved. This is Satan's counterfeit for the one true God, the Father of our Lord Jesus Christ. Deuteronomy 6:4 says, "The LORD our God, the LORD is one." In Ephesians 1:3 we read, "Praise be to the God and Father of our Lord Jesus Christ."

God is not an "it" or a "force." He is alive and our personal Lord and Savior. The Bible is filled with His attributes and they tell us what kind of a great and awesome God He really is.

3. You Are a Little God.

New Agers believe that since we are all gods, we must become "cosmically conscious" of the fact that we are gods. Jesus did that. He was nothing more than an enlightened master, something like good old Splinter with his buddies the Teenage Mutant Ninja Turtles. Jesus was a dynamic teacher and an incredible person because he came to grips with the fact that he was a little god. And just like Jesus, everyone else must come to realize that they, too, are gods and start living like it.

New Agers say, "We, too, share in the Christ-consciousness within us. The Savior out there is being replaced by the savior in us. There is no need for a Christ because we can save ourselves."

New Agers teach that reincarnation makes all this possible. The birth, death, rebirth process you go through over hundreds and even thousands of years helps you get in touch with your karma. The object is to keep correcting your mistakes through the various lifetimes until reaching a point of perfection where you become a god.

This principle is a counterfeit. The Bible teaches in Ephesians 2:8,9 that "you were saved by faith in God's kindness. This is God's gift to you and not anything you have done on your own" (CEV).

The Bible also says we are filled with hope as we wait for the glorious return of our great God and Savior, Jesus Christ (Titus 2:13). Jesus died on the cross to take the punishment for our sin. He paid our debt and died our death. Why? So we could experience new life and forgiveness for our sins. There is no second chance to come back and fix your mistakes. The Bible is very clear when it says we die only once and then we are judged (Hebrews 9:27).

4. We're Working Toward a New World Order.

New Agers believe the countries of the world are coming together and eventually national boundaries will no longer be necessary. People are all working to reach an omega point—ultimate peace. But it will only happen when we have a one-world government and a one-world religion.

Because of the unsettling world situation today, people are primed for someone to emerge as a leader, someone who has the answer for all our problems. Someone to lead the entire world. Ten nations in Europe are testing the idea of using one currency. Countries that were once divided are united again. New Agers see all this as ushering in a New World Order—a counterfeit for the kingdom of God.

The Bible teaches that only God will create a new heaven and earth (Isaiah 65:17). There will not be harmony or peace in this world until the Prince of Peace (Isaiah 9:6; 2 Thessalonians 3:16) comes to live in the hearts of people.

5. Reality Is What You Make It.

New Agers say reality is determined by what you believe, which is essentially the premise of virtual reality. If you change what you believe, you can change reality. Because reality is what you make it, there are no such things as moral absolutes or good and evil. Reality is what you think is good, even if someone else thinks it is evil.

A TV talk show host was interviewing the head of a very militant homosexual organization. This leader was pushing for their members to start having sex with young children under the age of five years old. The reporter was outraged and said so. The guest replied with, "Hey lady, that is my truth. And even though it isn't your truth, it doesn't matter what you think."

What about premarital sex? It's okay if you think it's okay. Just use a condom. Without moral absolutes, all sex is good sex, according to Dr. Ruth, even between people and animals—as long as you think it is good.

The world is now a huge potpourri of "anything goes." Everyone is developing their own ethics and codes of conduct, and the result is total confusion, total chaos. Research points out that the younger you are, the less you believe in absolute truth.

The sense of good and evil has been placed in our hearts by God (Romans 2:15). Without any sense of right and wrong, this world is going to become a jungle. Look at the havoc in the world today: rioting, race wars, ethnic cleansing, greed that brings about starvation, drive-by shootings. Is this really the kind of world you want to live in? It reminds me of a kingdom of animals.

John 8:32 says that when you know the truth, it will set you free. Jesus said in John 14:6, "I am the way and the truth and the life. No one comes to the Father except through me." Absolute truth comes from God. Satan is saying it is all relative.

In some of your classrooms it's called "values clarification." You need to look to the Bible as your standard for right and wrong, so you will know the difference.

6. We Have a New Way of Thinking.

New Agers believe we need to develop a new way of thinking about old problems. We need to think "holistically." If we are all interconnected particles in this cosmic ocean, and if we all are part of God, then we are able to think on one level. This new way of thinking only comes from a "mystical spiritual awakening" by getting in touch with your inner child.

But the Bible says we need to change the way we think by renewing our mind (Romans 12:2). We are capable of thinking only in human terms, but God can enable us to have an eternal perspective. Our new way of thinking also comes as a result of being new creations in Christ (2 Corinthians 5:17). The way to fully develop this new way of thinking is to allow God to readjust our minds, and this only happens through the study and knowledge of His Word.

The New Age is probably the most widespread and powerful phenomenon affecting our culture today. Its philosophy influences music, sports, literature—in fact, nothing seems exempt, not even some churches. In dealing with the New Age movement we are really dealing with spiritual warfare against the forces of darkness. And this aspect of the battle is being fought in our minds.

There are many dangers associated with the New Age, but the biggest danger of all is that it keeps people who are searching for spiritual truth from finding the real thing—a personal relationship with Jesus Christ.

Watch for the trap of New Age thinking. Stay informed as to what is out there, and stay close to the Lord and in His Word. Be on the alert for subtle influences of New Age thinking trying to creep into your mind as Satan attempts to get to you. And remember, with Christ you are on the winning side. Now stay tuned for Part 3, where we will learn to stand up to the devil.

Something to Think About

1. Beside each one of the six principles of New Age thinking, write at least one place in our culture where you can see that influence. Be specific.

   - All Is One. One Is All.
   - God Is Everything. Everything Is God.
   - You Are a Little God.
   - We're Working Toward a New World Order.
   - Reality Is What You Make It.
   - We Have a New Way of Thinking.

2. Read 1 Timothy 4:1,2. How do these verses relate to the New Age movement? Be specific.

3. New Agers are generally active in trying to address the problems in the world. As Christians, we should be even

more active in making a difference. What one thing can you do this week to help deal with a problem in your sphere of influence?

4. Why is it wrong for a Christian to believe in reincarnation? Find at least one verse to support your answer.

———————

PART THREE

Standing Up to the Devil

9

Take Control

I met Robert at a high school summer camp I was speaking at. He was into music—thrash, metal, and alternative—so because of my background in music we hit it off right away. As we talked I sensed something was really bothering Robert, but I wasn't able to figure out what it was.

Then on Thursday night I gave the group the opportunity to receive Christ. Robert was one of the first to stand up and indicate he had made a commitment. After the meeting was over, Robert's youth pastor asked if I could talk to Robert for a few minutes.

Robert opened up to me about how rough his life had been. He told me how he had been worshiping Satan after a friend convinced him his life would be better if he did. Robert explained how he and his friend got into all kinds of evil. They used marijuana and crystal methane. Together they studied the *Satanic Bible* and asked the Ouija board for answers about life. They also prayed to Satan for help about their problems.

But that week at camp changed everything. Every time I spoke, Robert would hear a strange voice in his head say, "I love you and want to make your life better. Don't listen to Steve." But Robert kept listening anyway—to every one of my messages. And he began to sense that something was missing in his life.

Finally on the night I gave the invitation to receive Christ, Robert realized that Jesus was missing from his life. At that point the voice in his head got violent and said, "If you turn to Christ, I'm going to kill you." Robert made the decision anyway, knowing it was the right thing to do. But he was frightened about what might happen.

I reassured Robert that he had done the right thing and that he could trust God to protect him. One of the first verses I shared with him was 1 John 4:4: "Children, you belong to God, and you have defeated these enemies. God's Spirit is in you and is more powerful than the one that is in the world" (CEV).

Robert realized that he had been living a lie for several years. He knew there would be a lot of changes happening now that he belonged to Jesus. Recently I talked with one of the staff members at Robert's church and found out Robert was still hanging in there on the commitment he had made at camp. It hadn't been easy, but it had definitely been worth it. Robert took a bold stand against the devil and won. And so can you.

You're not alone in the battle. God is ready and willing to help you. In these final chapters, we'll be talking about how to defend yourself against Satan's attacks. And we'll start with learning how to take control of your mind.

Prepare Your Mind for Battle

Beginning in 1931 and continuing for the next ten years, every graduating naval cadet in Japan was asked the same question: "How would you carry out a surprise attack on Pearl Harbor?" In February of 1932, the Japanese received an answer that they believed was a foolproof plan. And it actually was the strategy they eventually used.

In the fall of 1941, a Japanese ship arrived at Honolulu. Four members of the crew, posing as stewards, were really two submarine experts and two surface ship and air operations experts from the Japanese Imperial Navy.

Those four Japanese naval experts were testing a plan they had been counting on for almost ten years. Disguised as stewards, these officers took plenty of shore leave, saw the sights, took pictures, and even took tourist plane rides over Pearl Harbor—and more pictures. The consulate gave these Japanese "stewards" maps of Pearl Harbor and the military airfields. They even purchased souvenir sets of postcards containing aerial shots of Battleship Row and the docking area by Ford Island.

One month later a fleet of Japanese naval ships arrived in Hawaii, only this time it was for attack. On December 7, 1941, Japan took the United States military completely by surprise. In 110 minutes, eight large battleships and three light cruisers had been sunk or damaged, 188 planes had been destroyed, 2,400 men had been killed.

The attack not only paralyzed the U.S. military in the Pacific for almost a year, but it also exposed our unbelievable unreadiness for battle. An investigation later showed that soldiers manning a radar station early the morning of December 7 had actually seen the Japanese planes approaching Pearl Harbor. But because they were unprepared for a possible attack, these soldiers thought that what they were seeing on the radar screen was American planes and they failed to verify this with anyone else. By the time they realized what was really happening, it was too late. Had Pearl Harbor been on the alert and prepared for action, who knows how many lives could have been saved.

The damage Satan can cause in your life may not be in terms of casualties and equipment loss, but he can make you miserable, angry, and bitter. Are you prepared for action so this doesn't happen? Are you on the alert in your mind?

Here are some ideas to help you take control of your thoughts and win the battle for your mind.

Be on the Alert

I have a good friend who is a fireman. One late night I was on the phone with him at the fire station. In the middle of our conversation, the alarm at the station went off, indicating an emergency. Bill said, "Sorry, Steve. That sound means I gotta go. Talk with you later." And he was gone! During every shift that Bill works at the fire station, he must be alert and prepared for emergency action at any time—even in the middle of the night.

Are you prepared like that in the battle for your mind? First Peter 1:13 tells us to prepare our minds for action and be self-controlled. In other words, get serious about the spiritual battle for your mind. Put your mind on alert to everything that may obstruct clear and obedient thinking. Don't just sit around and see what happens. There's important work to be accomplished.

Be careful what you expose your mind to at all times. Don't forget Satan is subtle and masquerades as an angel of light (2 Corinthians 11:14). He will attack you from any direction and at any time. Being prepared means that you are not only ready for action, but that you possess the proper and necessary equipment for battle as well. (We'll talk more about this later in the chapters "Combat Ready" and "Choose Your Weapons.")

If you are prepared for action and on the alert, you will be able to protect your mind and what goes in it.

Guard Your Mind

While on a ministry trip to the Philippines, we stayed at a large, multistoried hotel. When we checked in, I noticed that there were armed guards everywhere. Twenty-four hours a day these guards stood at the front doors to the hotel, checking everyone who tried to enter. There were also guards on every floor of the hotel protecting the rooms. Each time we got off the elevator to head to our room, the guards would ask for our name and room number, and then they would write something in a record book. They were being extremely careful not to let anyone in the hotel or a room who didn't belong there.

The same principle should apply to our minds. Proverbs 4:23 says, "Above all else, guard your heart, for it is the wellspring of life." Generally speaking, the word for *heart* in this verse is referring to the mind—our purposes, intentions, understanding, and knowledge.

Because the devil assaults us from many directions with every conceivable form of evil, our minds must be strongly guarded. We must become aware of our weak points mentally—where we are vulnerable to evil enticements. Satan knows where we are vulnerable and looks for ways to influence our thinking.

Our goal should be to not let evil of any form in our minds, not giving the devil any kind of foothold in our thinking process. Our minds are constantly gathering and storing information, just like a video camera. We need to stop consuming anything and everything available to us for entertainment and recreation without recognizing that not all of it is good for our mental and spiritual well-being.

It's not easy to erase the videotapes of our minds. I'm not proud of some of the things I put into my mind before I was a Christian. And it's been amazing to me how Satan loves to do instant replays in my mind of some of these things. Closely guard what gets "recorded," because it may continue to influence your thinking long after you first saw or heard it.

If the fortress is taken, the entire town must surrender. If the mind is captured, the whole person—affections, desires, motives, and actions—is prisoner. Ultimately, to guard our minds means we must guard our eyes and ears because they are the potential entry points for evil.

Protecting our minds from what goes in is the first step toward changing our thinking.

Change the Way You Think

My car was running lousy, so I took it to the shop to have the problem fixed. The mechanic told me there were a couple of reasons why my car was running so poorly. The main reason, he said, had to do with the type of gas I was using—the octane level wasn't high enough. After his repairs and the change in gas, the car ran fine.

Sometimes our lives are not "running smoothly" because we are putting the wrong "fuel" in our minds. We need to change the input so we can change the way we think. But we can't do this alone. We need God's help.

The apostle Paul writes in Romans 12:2, "Don't be like the people of this world, but let God change the way you think. Then you will know how to do everything that is good and pleasing to him" (CEV).

God wants to change the control center of our attitudes, thoughts, feelings, and actions. This is accomplished when we have a steady input of God's Word, prayer, and meeting with other Christians. These things need to be a regular part of our life if we are to grow spiritually and have victory in the battle for our mind.

Have you made an adjustment in the things you put into your mind? Colossians 3:1,2 gives us this advice: "You have been raised to life with Christ. Now set your heart on what is in heaven, where Christ rules at God's right side. Think about what is up there, not about what is here on earth" (CEV). This does not mean we are to be so "heavenly bound, that we are no earthly good," but we are to model ourselves after Jesus and not the world.

Take Control

If we are going to be successful at staying alert, guarding our minds, and changing the way we think, we have to take control of our thoughts. God gives us a strategy for accomplishing this in 2 Corinthians 10:3-5:

> For though we live in the world, we do not wage war as the world does. The weapons we fight with are not the weapons of the world. On the contrary, they have divine power to demolish strongholds. We demolish arguments and every pretension that sets itself up against the knowledge of God, and we take captive every thought to make it obedient to Christ.

God wants us to run every thought through a "spiritual filtering system," find the ones that are against His truth, and destroy their influence in our lives by not allowing them into our minds.

The best filtering system is not Christian music or even what other Christians say—it's God's Word. The Bible is filled with many verses we can use to filter our thoughts so they are pleasing to God. Philippians 4:8 is one of the easiest verses to apply as a filter for our thinking (see Chapter 4, "The Battle for Your Mind").

When we filter, we compare what goes into our mind with God's Word to see if it is something we should think about. If it isn't, we immediately "tune" it out or "turn" it off. By using the Word of God, we are not dealing with someone else's opinion but with the source of all truth. And when we fill our minds with truth, we live the truth and not the devil's lies.

But why would you have to filter *every* thought? Look at it this way. How much poison does it take to harm you? Just a few drops. Satan doesn't need a whole lot of poisonous ideas to get a foothold in your life through your mind.

Have you ever wondered why you struggle with certain attitudes toward your parents or a friend, or why you have to take 18 cold showers before you go on a date to control your passion, or why you do some of the other things you do? It all has to do with what you've been putting in your mind.

The most effective way to utilize this "filtering system" is to keep it with you all the time. While we can't always carry a Bible around with us every place we go, we can memorize verses that apply to the mind (like Philippians 4:8) so that the filter is always in place and ready to use. By hiding God's Word in your heart (Psalm 119:11), your mind is always on alert. When something makes an attempt to infiltrate your thoughts, the filtering system is there to help you keep out harmful things.

And it really does work!

My ministry team and I were in Stockholm, Sweden, for a day and a half on our way home from a campaign in the Soviet Commonwealth. A couple of guys from the team and I decided to go see a movie. After a brief search we discovered a theater that was showing two films in English—a British version of *Robin Hood* and *Predator 2*. All of us were in the mood for an action film, and one of the guys thought that Arnold Schwarzenegger was the star in *Predator 2*. So we bought the tickets and went inside.

We quickly realized that we had confused *Terminator 2* with *Predator 2*. There was more sex, occultic violence, and gore in the first 15 minutes of the movie than I had seen in a long, long time. As I watched, I just kept thinking it was going to get better. But it didn't. Finally my spiritual filtering system clicked in, and a little voice in my mind said, "Hey, Russo. This isn't true, pure, right, holy, friendly, or proper. So stop putting this stuff in your mind and leave."

My next thought was, *What will my friends think?* Then I realized it didn't matter what they thought. I knew what I had to do to protect my mind. I told the other guys that I couldn't watch anymore, and I walked out. After I explained to the manager why I left, he said I could get my money back or go see *Robin Hood* instead. Within a few minutes my friends left *Predator 2* and joined me to watch *Robin Hood*. Filtering worked for me, and it can work for you.

It's okay to filter. There's nothing wrong with leaving a movie that's bad, or turning off a television show that's raunchy, or stopping the VCR if the movie you've rented isn't really something you should be watching, or even changing the radio to a more positive tune. Society (including some of your friends!) may think it's odd, but lining up with what God says about what we should be thinking about makes it a very wise thing to do.

Filtering isn't always easy, but it is worth it. You may take some heat from family or friends, but God will honor your decision. He may also use you to set an example for others about how important it is to guard your mind. When you find yourself in a position of having to stop watching or listening to something, don't make a big scene. Just quietly do whatever needs to be done (walk out, leave the room, etc.). Then if someone asks why you left, in a nonjudgmental way explain to them that what you were doing with everyone else wasn't right for you, that you have made a choice to be more selective in your entertainment. If you take a positive approach to sharing your convictions, it may open the door for you to explain more of the "why" with your friends, including a chance to tell them about Jesus.

Take the "Russo Challenge"

Here's something I want you to consider. I call it the "Russo Challenge." For one week don't turn on the stereo, watch TV, go to a movie, or play a computer or video game. In other words, turn it all off—even if it's Christian. Use the time you normally would with the "entertainment thing" to get into God's Word. Take time to pray and turn to God for answers to questions in your life. Give the Lord a chance to really clean out your mind and change your thinking without any competition.

You'll be amazed at the changes. Your attitudes about certain things, people, and life will be different. You will notice a new sense of self-control and peace. And you will take on a more hopeful perspective about your problems in life. All of this and more will take place because you will be much more aware of God's perspective rather than the world's.

During week two of the Russo Challenge, don't tune into music, turn on the TV, or pop in a game cartridge until you've been in the Word. To help you remember, take several 3x5 cards and print in big, bold letters WORD on each one. Place them in your room, locker, car—anywhere you will see them frequently each day. And not having enough time is not a valid excuse. No matter how busy we get, we always find time to do what we want to do.

If you're not sure where to start reading, why not choose something from the Old Testament and something from the New? In the Old Testament, start with the book of Proverbs. There is one chapter of Proverbs for every day of the month, so you'll never forget where you are supposed to be. Then in the New Testament start with one of the gospels: Matthew, Mark, Luke, or John. Read a chapter a day. Each week find a verse that really hits home for you and memorize it. Write it out on a 3x5 card so you can carry it around with you as you work on it. And don't forget to spend at least five minutes a day in prayer. (See the chapter "Choose Your Weapons" for more help.)

After you complete the second week, continue doing the same thing for the next two weeks that follow. There's no telling how dramatically your life may change if you get serious about taking control of your mind!

Finally, here are a couple more things to consider regarding the Russo Challenge. First, why not put the challenge to family members and friends? Your example may be all they need. Second, write to me if you take the challenge, and let me know the results. I want to be able to encourage you in the stand you have taken. You will find my address in the back of the book.

Nothing is more important than taking control of your mind. That's where the battle is not only waged, but where it will be won or lost! Reread this chapter if necessary, and put the things we have discussed into practice. God is more than willing to help us, but we have to make an effort to be obedient to the truth of His Word. Nothing has greater potential to change our lives than winning the battle for our mind.

Get serious and just do it!

Something to Think About

1. Read Isaiah 26:3 and Philippians 4:7. What are some of the benefits to keeping your mind focused on God?

2. What areas of your thought life need to be renewed?

3. Read Matthew 22:37. What steps are you taking to fulfill the commandment of loving God with all your mind?

10

Our Defender

Shortly after talking about kids and Satanism on the national radio program "Focus on the Family," I received a call from a counselor at a local high school. She was deeply concerned about the number of students on campus who were dabbling with Satanism and the occult. More than 150 teens had been referred for professional counseling in the first six weeks of school because of their involvement. "You must do something to help us," she pleaded. "The problem is getting worse."

"Could you give me a profile of the typical student who is involved?" I asked.

Without any hesitation she responded, "They're all churched kids. I think they've been given a taste of the supernatural but have never been given the real thing."

We're used to hearing about the real thing in soft drink ads, but this time we're talking about Jesus—our ally, our defender. Do you really know Him? I'm talking about the Jesus of the Bible, not the Jesus whose name is thrown around the locker room or mocked in some movie. Let's look at a couple of examples of how mixed up people can get when it comes to Jesus.

I was speaking about Jesus at a girls' unit in the Los

Angeles County juvenile hall. After finishing, I was talking with one of the girls. "Y'all think this Jesus is lord and king. But I know better," she blurted out. "He ain't nothing but a homeboy. He's just like the other homeys on my street and in my neighborhood." This girl had no clue who Jesus really is, and yet He's the only One who can help her straighten her life out.

Another time I was speaking to a group of youth pastors and youth workers at a special training seminar on reaching young people today. As we discussed the most effective way to tell teenagers about Jesus, I reminded the audience how important it was not to reduce the Lord to something less than what He really is. I went on to say that in our attempts to show how Jesus can relate to students, we have gone too far with things like "Jesus the metal head" or "Jesus the rapper" or even "Jesus the homeboy." The Jesus of the Bible transcends all that and already is incredibly relevant to the lives of young people today.

One of the youth pastors in the audience spoke up and said that he totally disagreed with what I was saying. He explained that the only Jesus kids in his neighborhood would accept is "Jesus the homeboy." And before he could even share Jesus with his kids, he needed to help them feel good about themselves culturally.

I couldn't believe what I was hearing. No wonder it's so hard for some people to understand who Jesus really is when that's what they are being taught! This guy had it all backwards, sideways, and messed up. Jesus isn't a metal head, a rapper, or a homeboy. He's the Son of God. And the only way young people will ever feel good about themselves is when they find their true identity in Christ (we'll talk more about this in the next chapter).

Maybe you've already come to the conclusion that Jesus is more than a homeboy, but do you know Him as Lord of lords and King of kings? One of the most important factors in standing up to the devil is to really know the One you've placed your faith in, the One who conquered death and made a new life possible.

Who Is Jesus?

Who do you say Jesus is? This is the most crucial question in life. The way we answer this question will spell the difference between life and death, the difference between a meaningful life and a meaningless one.

Almost 2,000 years ago Jesus entered the human race. He was born in a barn in a small Jewish town to a poor family. He never wrote a book, had a family, or went to college. He never traveled more than 200 miles from his birthplace and only lived 33 years. Yet despite His rather humble existence, Jesus lived the most influential life of anyone ever.

Jesus was the most unique person who ever lived. He was both completely God and completely man. His life was marked with things that completely set Him apart from anyone else.

No one ever said what Jesus said. He claimed that He was God (John 8:19; 10:30; 14:9). He also said that He had the authority to forgive sins for eternity (Mark 2:1-12) and that He was the only way to God (John 14:6).

No one ever lived like Jesus lived. He was born of a virgin (Matthew 1:20) with no place to call home. He healed the sick and gave sight to the blind (Mark 1:33,34; John 9). His life was perfect and without sin (Hebrews 4:15). And He lived to give us life abundantly and eternally (John 10:10,28). Jesus Christ was the perfect model for the rest of humanity in what it meant to be totally dependent on God.

Jesus Defeated Satan

We can have confidence in Jesus and victory in spiritual warfare because He defeated Satan through His life, death, and resurrection. Jesus is not only our protector but He also is the greatest conqueror ever!

Jesus Defeated Satan Through His Life

How Jesus lived defeated Satan. A prime example of this is found in Matthew 4:1-11:

> The Holy Spirit led Jesus into the desert, so that the devil could test him. After Jesus went without eating for forty days and nights, he was very hungry. Then the devil came to him and said, "If you are God's Son, then tell these stones to turn into bread." Jesus answered, "The Scriptures say: 'No one can live only on food. People need every word that God has spoken.'"

> Next, the devil took Jesus to the holy city and had him stand on the highest part of the temple. The devil said, "If you are God's Son, jump off. The Scriptures say: 'God will give his angels orders about you. They will catch you in their arms, and will not hurt your feet on the stones.'" Jesus answered, "The Scriptures also say, 'Don't try to test the Lord your God!'"

> Finally, the devil took Jesus up on a very high mountain and showed him all the kingdoms on earth and their power. The devil said to him, "I will give all this to you, if you will bow down and worship me." Jesus answered, "Go away

Satan! The Scriptures say: 'Worship the Lord
your God and serve only him.'" Then the devil
left Jesus, and the angels came to help him
(CEV).

Satan tempted Jesus in three main ways: physical, spiritual, and psychological. First, Jesus was enticed to meet His
physical needs apart from God. Living independent of God
is sin. Satan wanted Jesus to trust in Himself and not rely on
anyone else—including God.

In the second temptation Satan dared Jesus to test God.
But Jesus knew that even though the devil supported his
temptation with Scripture, he was only quoting part of the
passage from Psalm 91:11,12. Satan left out the most important part that tells us that the angels will help to keep us
from stumbling in the first place. Jesus also knew that
exposing yourself to danger needlessly is a way of testing
God, and this goes against the principle of faith we are to
live by.

In the third temptation the devil offered Jesus all the
kingdoms of the world—if Jesus would just worship him.
Satan psychologically tempted Jesus with power. But Jesus
knew that God is the only one who should be worshiped and
served.

Jesus was able to stand up to the devil against every
temptation by living a life in obedience to God and His
Word. The way Jesus lived His life gave Him the ability to
defeat Satan. And the same can be true for us. It all comes
back to knowing God's Word and obeying it.

Jesus Defeated Satan Through His Death

From the time of Christ's birth, Satan did all in his
power to bring about Jesus' downfall. But he was doomed to
fail. The Bible says in 1 John 3:8c, "The reason the Son

of God appeared was to destroy the devil's work." This happened through Christ's death on the cross and His resurrection. No one ever died like Jesus died. His death on the cross was different (Mark 8:31). He took on the sins of the world and suffered the punishment that we deserved (Isaiah 53:6). He was our substitute so we could be forgiven. Jesus died so we could live.

On the cross Jesus destroyed the fear of death which Satan had used to enslave people from the beginning of time. In Hebrews 2:14,15 we read about Christ's destruction of the devil's hold on us:

> Since the children have flesh and blood, he too shared in their humanity so that by his death he might destroy him who holds the power of death—that is, the devil—and free those who all their lives were held in slavery by their fear of death.

Satan is now just a shadow of what he once was. He and his army have been stripped of their power. And for those who trust in Christ, the power Satan once had is now completely ineffective, eternal life is guaranteed, and the fear of physical death is gone. All because of Jesus' death on the cross.

Jesus Defeated Satan Through His Resurrection

By far, the greatest thing that is totally unique about Jesus is His resurrection. It is the most important part of the gospel or "good news."

After Jesus' body was taken off the cross, it was placed in a borrowed tomb. Three days later He came back to life and gave many people convincing proof that He was alive (Acts 1:3). All of Christianity stands or falls on the resurrection of Jesus Christ. The Bible puts it this way: "If there is no resurrection of the dead, then not even Christ has been raised. And if Christ has not been raised, our preaching is useless and so is your faith" (1 Corinthians 15:13,14).

The word *resurrection* in the Bible is defined as "the standing up of a body." The resurrection of Jesus was not just spiritual, but physical as well. Jesus' body literally "stood up" from death back to life. When the Bible says Jesus gave "convincing proof" He was alive, it was speaking of physical life, not just some "spirit being" walking around.

According to many scholars, there is no historic event better supported by the evidence than the resurrection of Jesus Christ. Jesus was brought back to life in time and space by the supernatural power of God as proof that He is exactly who He says He is, and so that we would be acceptable to God in spite of our sin (Romans 4:25).

In His death Jesus took away our sins, and in His resurrection He gave us a guaranteed entrance to heaven. Because of the resurrection we have hope. And this hope gives meaning and purpose to life. So many people today lack direction for their lives because they don't know Jesus. Life without Christ is a hopeless end; life with Christ is an endless hope.

The good news is that this same power is available to you and me to help us face the struggles and overcome the pain of life. Jesus Christ is alive and is sufficient to meet all your needs.

Where Our Victory Comes From

Even though Satan is a defeated foe, the spiritual battle will continue until the day we exit this life and go to be with Jesus. Victory in the battle can be ours by daily submitting to Christ and acknowledging Him as Lord.

When you go to a doctor for medical care, you submit yourself to him. You may not always agree with what he says or prescribes, but you obey him (most of the time!). You take the medicine, even if it tastes gross, because the doctor is the boss at that moment of time, and he knows what's best.

To submit to Christ means we must willfully surrender to God and take a stand against the devil. It means we want God's desires for our life more than we want our own. Instead of resisting God's will for us, we should resist the devil. We acknowledge Him as Lord (the boss) because He created us and knows what is best for us.

If we submit to God and resist the devil, the Bible says he will flee from us (James 4:7). The devil can be resisted. Jesus was our example, and it is by His resurrection power that we can stand up against Satan.

Make it a priority to spend time each day developing your relationship with Jesus. Get to know the "real thing" so when the counterfeit—our enemy—attacks, you will recognize him. Dig in and study God's Word, especially the four gospels—Matthew, Mark, Luke, and John. These books give us a great picture of who Jesus is, what He was like, and how He related to other people.

As you get to know Jesus, you can't help but love Him. And the more you love Him, the more you will want to please Him. The closer you get to Jesus and live the truth, the more easily you will see the lie that Satan is trying to get you to believe. But all this takes time. You will have to change some of your priorities.

Think about your other relationships. If you never spent any time with your friends and family, what kind of relationships would you have? You know those people because you spend time with them. And the same is true with Jesus. Once you really know the "real thing," you won't want the counterfeit! Take time to get to know Jesus now before the devil really starts to turn up the heat. You'll never regret it.

Jesus is not just any other religious leader. He is the Son of God, Lord of lords, and your defender. The Lord is on your side and wants you to win at life. Think about it: If Jesus is for you, who could possibly be against you?

———————

Something to Think About

1. What is the difference between knowing about Jesus and really knowing Him? Be specific.

2. Who first told you about Jesus? How was He described to you? What about Him did you find appealing at first? What about now?

3. What areas of your life are the most difficult to submit to God? Why?

4. What temptation(s) is the devil putting before you that is difficult for you to resist? What changes do you need to make in your life so you will be able to stand up to the devil and experience victory in the spiritual battle in these areas?

———————

11

Who Are You?

Hook is a nineties version of Peter Pan. Peter Pan is grown-up now and known as corporate executive officer Peter Banning. He has all the toys that a CEO possesses: expensive car, cellular phone, and power suits. His life is so wrapped up in the corporate world that he doesn't have a whole lot of time for his family or even himself.

Peter, his wife, and two children make a trip to England to visit Granny Wendy, the woman who raised him. A new wing of a children's home is going to be named after her, and there is a special dinner being held in Granny Wendy's honor.

On the night of the banquet, Peter's son and daughter are kidnapped. The abductor tacks a note on the door of the children's room with a dagger. The message is from Captain Hook, challenging Peter to the ultimate duel over his children in Never-Never Land.

Peter Banning soon faces a double crisis: His children are gone and Granny Wendy tells him that he must come to grips with his true identity—Peter Pan—in order to rescue his children. But Peter rebels against this new knowledge because he doesn't want to accept who he really is.

Tinkerbell then visits Peter in the middle of the night

and carries him off to Never-Never Land. He experiences a fascinating adventure, but he's also working through a tremendous identity crisis. Tinkerbell and the Lost Boys tell Peter that he must try to remember who he really is, and the only way this will happen is by recalling a happy memory. His happy memory finally comes to him—when he became a father for the first time.

Suddenly Peter's life is totally transformed. He now believes and understands who he really is, and his life takes on new meaning. He is able to defeat Captain Hook and rescue his children. All of them eventually return home together from Never-Never Land and live happily ever after.

Knowing who you are is the key to a meaningful life. When we come to grips with who we are, our whole perspective on life radically changes. But many people don't know how to find their identity (it takes more than a happy memory!), and when they do, they don't want to believe it. They are afraid they might become someone they don't want to be.

Do you know who you are?

How Not to Determine Who You Are

Telling me your name, where you live or go to school, or what you like to do are things about you. But even with all that information, you still haven't told me who you really are.

Who we are is not determined by what we do, where we live or go to school, or even what we possess. I remember meeting a high school student who introduced himself to me and immediately told me that he owned a 1968 Cougar. He went on for more than 20 minutes talking about his car. He told me every detail imaginable!

I wanted to interrupt him and say, "Time out. Are you trying to tell me who you are, or are you telling me about something you own? There seems to be some confusion here."

When I was in high school I did well in academics and sports, but more than anything I was into music. It was my life. So when I went to my high school class reunion, people thought I was still doing the music gig. They would come up to me and say, "Hey, Russo. What's happening? Who are you playing with and recording with now?" When I responded that I was in the ministry now, they didn't know what to do with me. It was almost as if I told them I had some strange tropical disease that was highly contagious. They politely said bye and took off to another part of the room. During all those years in school everyone had my identity wrapped up in the drums. And so did I.

The misconception over identity can work the opposite way also. If you can't perform or you don't have the status or possessions the world says you need, you begin to think of yourself as worthless. You see yourself as a loser because you didn't make good grades in a particular class or you didn't make a certain team. Or maybe you have been hearing for a long time from your parents, teachers, or friends that you'll never succeed in anything.

I took a speech class my freshman year of college, and one day after class the professor asked to speak to me privately. "There's one thing I want to encourage you to never consider as a profession," she said. "Public speaking. You just don't have what it takes." That's funny, isn't it? I speak to groups all over the world! I would like to find that professor now and let her know what God can do in a person's life.

Have you discovered your identity? Do you really know who you are? Who you are is determined by much more than what you have, what you do, and what you achieve.

Many years ago there was an Olympic athlete named Keith Wegeman. He was an amazing ski jumper. From the time he was able to get on a set of skis as a child, all he wanted to do was make it to the Olympics. He competed through the years and eventually found himself in the winter Olympics. He was competing against the best of the best from all over the world. And he won! He was *the* best, and he got the gold.

Yet in spite of his tremendous victory, the celebration didn't last. Something hit him like a ton of bricks: He had nothing left to live for anymore. He had achieved it all. Everything he ever hoped to be, everything he ever dreamed of achieving, had been accomplished.

He was so disillusioned that he even considered suicide. He basically sat and watched his life waste away—until somebody finally shared with him how things were really just beginning. Keith's friends helped him discover who he really was.

The way to know our true identity is by opening our lives to Jesus Christ as our Savior and Lord. It is only in Christ that we find out who we are. And that is what finally happened to Keith. He was confronted with and came to love the One who knew him better than anyone else, even better than he knew himself. He found out about the One who put him together, piece by piece, molecule by molecule, in his mother's womb. In Jesus his true identity was found. And this knowledge totally transformed Keith's life.

How about you? Have you come to grips with who you are in Christ? Do you know He loves you just for *you?* That in His eyes you're somebody special? Billions and billions of people have been born and walked the face of this planet, yet there have never been any two who are exactly alike, not even identical twins. That famous author "Anonymous" wrote some words that describe this fact perfectly. After you read, take a minute to let the message really soak in.

I'm Special

I'm special. In all the world there's nobody like me. Since the beginning of time, there has never been another person like me. Nobody has my smile. Nobody has my eyes, my nose, my hair, my hands, my voice. I'm special.

No one can be found who has my handwriting. Nobody anywhere has my tastes—for food or music or art. No one sees things just as I do. In all of time there's been no one who laughs like me, no one who cries like me. And what makes me laugh and cry will never provoke identical laughter and tears from anybody else, ever. No one reacts to any situation just as I would react. I'm special.

I'm the only one in all of creation who has my set of abilities. Oh, there will always be somebody who is better at one of the things I'm good at, but no one in the universe can reach my combination of talents, ideas, abilities, and feelings. Like a room full of musical instruments, some may excel alone, but none can match the symphony sound when all are played together. I'm a symphony.

Through all of eternity no one will ever look, talk, walk, think, or do like me. I'm special. I'm rare.

And, in all rarity there is great value. Because of my great rare value, I need not attempt to imitate others. I will accept—yes, celebrate—my differences. I'm special.

And I'm beginning to realize it's no accident that I'm special. I'm beginning to see that God made me special for a very special purpose.

He must have a job for me that no one else can do as well as I. Out of all the billions of applicants, only one is qualified, only one has the right combination of what it takes.

That one is me. Because . . . I'm special.

Now that you are beginning to realize just how special you are, let's take a closer look at how to develop your true identity.

Your True Identity

In the Bible we learn that if anyone is in Christ, he is a new creation. The old has gone and the new has come (2 Corinthians 5:17). When you open your heart and life to Jesus Christ, you become a brand-new person, a person who has never existed before. The apostle Paul writes in Ephesians 5:8, "For you were once darkness, but now you are light in the Lord. Live as children of light." There isn't anything more dramatically different than darkness and light. This is how different your life will be once you recognize who you are.

Unfortunately, this concept is somewhat misunderstood today. I'd like to clear up some of the confusion. To begin with, did you know that there are two births you can have in life? A physical one and a spiritual one. When we are born physically, the result is physical life. When we are "born again" spiritually, we receive eternal life.

When we are born spiritually, it opens up all the other dimensions of our life—social, emotional, physical, intellectual—enabling us to become the people God has designed us to be. That one missing piece ultimately makes sense out of life. A new life in Christ gives you a brand-new identity. Becoming a Christian is not just something you add to your life—it becomes your life. You may look the same on the outside, but you are a radically different person on the inside.

As a Christian you are a brand-new person. God has given you a new heart. You have been *completely* forgiven of all your sin and given a new start at life. That means you can stop living under the cloud of guilt the devil is attempting to put over you about your past. Start experiencing life as the person God designed you to be. And you have not only had your sin debt paid in full, but you've been given an awesome power to overcome the challenges in life as well. Let the resurrection power of Jesus help you win.

Life isn't always easy, especially in the world today. Broken families, money problems, abuse, and hopelessness can get you down. Things get even more complicated when you add the spiritual battle that is raging in our lives. Don't get too bummed out, though. Instead, stand up to the devil and the philosophies of the world, and start enjoying life God's way!

Jesus said, "I came that everyone would have life, and have it to its fullest" (John 10:10 CEV). The Lord wants you to get the most out of life. When you have secured your destiny and identity through Christ, it should affect the quality of life you live here on earth. There will always be problems, pressures, and stress, but the way you respond is going to be different because you now have all the resources of the living God transforming your life and giving you victory over the daily struggles.

It's critically important to realize that we are not the same people after we come to Christ that we once were. Now you may be thinking to yourself, "Steve, I gave my life to Jesus and I'm *still* struggling with my identity and my self-image." Then you have been deceived by the devil. He has distorted the truth about your identity. Stop listening to the lies of the enemy and start living the truth. Satan would have you believe that you are nothing more than a rotten sinner who is saved by grace. While it's true that we are saved by grace, that there is nothing we can possibly do to save ourselves (Ephesians 2:8,9), God no longer sees us as sinners but rather as saints who are struggling with sin and the temptations of this world (Ephesians 1:1). This is part of our new identity.

God changes us so completely in Christ that even He looks at us differently. The Bible teaches that we are God's workmanship created in Christ Jesus to do good works which God prepared in advance for us to do (Ephesians 2:10). God designed us to do good things—to win at life!

Meaning and purpose in life cannot be found outside of Jesus. Stop chasing the soap bubbles of this world that Satan is blowing in your path. You are a child of God. Live in an appropriate way. John 1:12 tells us, "Yet to all who received him, to those who believed in his name, he gave the right to become children of God." Since our Father in heaven is the Lord of lords and the King of kings, what does that make us? That makes us children of the King. Talk about feeling significant! Are you living like the royalty that you really are?

Ephesians 4:1 puts it another way: "I urge you to live a life worthy of the calling you have received." What happens when Prince Charles of England goes anywhere? How is he treated? People literally roll out the red carpet for him. Heads of state and bands greet him. People take extra-special care of him. He even has bodyguards for protection. Why? Because he is the son of royalty and the future king of England.

But just think, if you know Jesus you have more of a heritage and an inheritance than Prince Charles. You are a child of the King of the heavens and will rule forever with the Lord of all creation.

The Bible's Descriptions of
Who We Are in Christ

The Bible is filled with incredible descriptions of our identity in Jesus Christ. Let's take a look at some of the passages that can help us get an even better idea of who we really are.

In 1 Corinthians 6:19,20 we read: "You are not your own, you were bought at a price." What was the cost of buying our freedom from the powers of darkness? We were bought with the very life of God's only Son, Jesus. God paid the highest price possible so our relationship with Him could be restored and our true identity secured. Isn't it amazing how valuable we are to God?

Knowing that we were bought with such a price should cause us to be more careful in the things we get involved in. You no longer have to "loan yourself out" and sell out your values to things like sex before marriage, gangs, or even chemical abuse just to feel worth something. You don't have to compromise any longer to gain love from anyone else. God wants you and will provide for your needs—even socially. You were bought with the ultimate price, so live with a sense of worth and value.

Colossian 1:13 describes the security that is part of our identity: "He has rescued us from the dominion of darkness and brought us into the kingdom of the Son he loves." Before we knew Christ, you and I were held as hostages of the devil to do his will (2 Timothy 2:26). We were prisoners, but God set us free! And Jesus said that once we were His, no one could take us from Him (John 10:28).

Do you remember Terry Anderson? He was a news correspondent in the Middle East who was taken captive by a militant religious group. He was held prisoner for a number of years under terrible conditions. When he was finally released, the celebration was fantastic. It seemed like the whole world partied!

But did you know that there is even a greater celebration for those who are set free from the captivity of Satan? Look at the words of Jesus in Luke 15:7: "In the same way there is more happiness in heaven because of one sinner who turns to God than over ninety-nine good people who don't need to" (CEV). When someone accepts Jesus in his or her heart, it's party time in heaven! Spiritual freedom is eternal freedom and security.

Next time you're feeling insecure because of friends or a family situation, stop and think about your security in Christ. Let this knowledge about your true identity influence your behavior. There is no need to fear anything that life may throw at you. The Bible says that God has not given us a spirit of fear, but one of power, love, and a sound mind (2 Timothy 1:7). Knowing Christ really can make a difference in the way you live.

Isn't it amazing how many dimensions of our life our identity (or lack of it) affects?

In Jesus we have everything we will ever need to make life worth living. That's not to say we don't need other relationships or a fulfilling career, but without knowing who we are in Christ, they are meaningless. Ephesians 1:3 says that we have been blessed with every spiritual blessing. Our minds can't even begin to comprehend what God has blessed us with or what He has planned for us. Don't miss what you already have in Christ by continuing to search for more in the wrong places.

Knowing Who We Are
Affects How We Behave

The more I think about our identity in Christ and what that means in our day-to-day lives, the more I'm convinced that we would see some of the problems that attack students today diminish and disappear altogether.

For example, the teen sex crisis. Over three million students every year get a sexually transmitted disease, including AIDS. And the number-one age group who will get hit by AIDS in the next five years will be high school students. Cities are passing out condoms on campus, but it isn't helping deal with the root of the problem. Some students tell me they are cutting holes in their condoms or not using them at all. Teenagers are having sex because they want to feel loved, accepted, and significant (everybody does). And they are attempting to gain all those things through a physical relationship.

Sex outside of marriage only causes scars and emotional pain. Satan lies and says it will make you feel loved, accepted, and significant, but it won't. Sex is a very special gift from God for married couples, and it is being misused with tragic results in our society. I believe if we help students understand who they are and that they have security, acceptance, and significance in *Christ*, it will reduce the number of teens who are sexually active. In Christ, you can have the confidence in yourself not to give in to the pressures of sexual temptation.

Another example of problems caused by the identity crisis is drug and alcohol (the number-one drug of choice) abuse. Alcohol-related traffic accidents kill more teenagers each year than any other thing. Why do people drink and do drugs? Sometimes to get others to like them and to feel part of what is going on. Sometimes it's a way of dealing with the pain and disappointment in life.

Once again, if students were able to grab hold of who they really are in Jesus Christ and all that God has designed for them to be and experience, I believe we would see this problem of drug and alcohol abuse greatly decrease.

And I'm sure you're aware of the explosive problem with gangs throughout the country. Gang members are in search of a sense of family, acceptance, security, and love. They may find these things with other gang bangers, but it's only temporary. It still doesn't get to the root of the problem—the need for a relationship with Christ.

The answer to the gang problem is to help students from all walks of life and every color understand who they can be in Jesus Christ and how to come to grips with their true identity.

I could fill page after page with crises from the youth culture—*your* culture—which find their roots in the identity issue. We could talk about bulimia, suicidal tendencies, and feelings of emptiness, and we would keep coming back to the fact that knowing who we are affects how we behave. I don't want to sound overly simplistic, but so many problems today could be solved by helping people find their true identity and letting that influence the way they live.

The only place you are going to find your real identity is in a vital, living relationship with Jesus Christ. This happens by surrendering your heart and life to Him, and saying, "Jesus, I want You to invade my humanity and help me to become the person I was designed to be so I can live my life to the fullest."

Some of the most frequent questions students ask me as I travel are, "What is life all about? Why am I here? How do I make my life count?" All of these and more can be answered in one word—Jesus. Satan will try to deceive you into not believing this awesome truth. He started doing this back in the beginning of human history with the first man and woman, and he hasn't changed his strategy since. Deception is his greatest weapon, especially when it comes to our identity. Satan knows all too well that the truth about who you are is the thing that will set you free. Jesus said He is the truth (John 14:6) and He is the way to freedom. Lasting security, acceptance, and significance will only be found in Christ.

Find yourself in Him and your life will never be the same. And remember this simple truth: Satan has come to take from you; Jesus has come to give to you.

Something to Think About

1. How do you find your true identity? Read John 3:1-3.

2. Take a 3x5 card and write the following on it: "I Am a Child of the King." Then put this card someplace where you will see it several times each day (on your dresser, desk, or on a mirror). This will be a small reminder of who you really are.

3. Have you ever felt inadequate and wished you were someone else? Why? How could understanding your identity help in this situation?

4. What is a Christian?

12

Combat Ready

A professional soldier's success in war is due to his preparation and his equipment. It would be suicidal to step into the heat of battle ill-equipped and unprepared. Tragically, many Christians today have not yet realized that we are also soldiers in the most intensive and crucial battle ever fought. Each day we face a brutal and fierce enemy. Many times we stumble home beaten up, wounded, and discouraged because we have not prepared ourselves for battle.

The battle in the student's world includes physical and sexual abuse, emotional harm, loneliness, stress, lack of purpose, drug and alcohol abuse, premarital sex, abortion, broken families, bulimia, and gangs. It's not easy to grow up in a world of confusing messages that kick you when you're down.

And the one who is behind so much of this pain is relentless. The enemy doesn't want to let go. His ultimate objective is to destroy us (John 10:10). But before you start feeling too overwhelmed, remember the devil is going "down for the count." Jesus not only beat Satan up, but also mortally wounded him on the cross.

God has made it possible for us to not only protect ourselves from the evil one's attack but also to have victory in the spiritual battle. In Ephesians 6, the apostle Paul gives us a detailed description of the spiritual armor God has given us. This armor can withstand every spiritual attack and is all the protection we need to defend ourselves from Satan and his evil schemes.

The apostle Paul lived during the time of the Roman empire, and he used the image of a Roman soldier as his model when he wrote to the church at Ephesus about the armor of God. The secret to the success of these seemingly invincible Roman warriors was in their preparation. In much the same way, God wants us to learn the importance of preparing for our battles by putting on our spiritual armor:

> Therefore put on the full armor of God, so that when the day of evil comes, you may be able to stand your ground, and after you have done everything, to stand. Stand firm then, with the belt of truth buckled around your waist, with the breastplate of righteousness in place, and with your feet fitted with the readiness that comes from the gospel of peace. In addition to all this, take up the shield of faith, with which you can extinguish all the flaming arrows of the evil one. Take the helmet of salvation and the sword of the Spirit, which is the word of God. And pray in the Spirit on all occasions with all kinds of prayers and requests (Ephesians 6:13-18).

Let's look more closely at each piece of the armor and see how it applies to our daily life.

Belt of Truth

The first piece of equipment Paul mentions is the belt. The soldier's belt, usually made out of leather, belonged to his underwear rather than to his armor, yet it was still an essential part of his equipment. It gathered his tunic (outer garment or robe) together and also held his sword in place. Buckling it on gave him a sense of hidden strength and confidence. He was prepared for action. If a soldier lost his belt, he lost everything.

The Christian soldier's belt is truth. We need to be convinced of the truth of the gospel and what it affirms in our lives as children of God. This means we need to have a genuine commitment to Christ and truthfulness. Hypocrisy, lying, and deceit have no place in the life of a follower of Christ. Our lives should be characterized by integrity and sincerity.

The devil is the father of lies and uses many schemes to mislead, deceive, and trick. The bottom line is that we need to know who we believe in and what we believe. Are you absolutely convinced that Jesus is the Son of God? Do you know what you believe about Him? Do you know the basics of your faith? If you are not certain, you are already defeated.

Make sure you are clear on who Jesus is and what the Bible teaches. It's not enough to believe. Make sure you believe *God's* truth. Then let His truth control your desires and direct the way you live. Remember, if Satan can get you to believe a lie, no matter how small, he can get you to live it. God's truth helps us to overcome Satan's lies.

Do you know what you believe? Could you defend your faith in a reasonable way to one of your teachers or to a skeptical relative? Do you really believe that God wants the best for you? Keep the belt of God's truth firmly buckled in your life.

Breastplate of Righteousness

The soldier's second piece of armor was the breastplate. It was often made of strong metal and shaped to fit a soldier's

upper body, usually front and back. The breastplate pro-
tected the vital organs (heart and lungs) and the stomach
(intestines) from the enemy's weapons.

During the apostle Paul's time, people thought that the
heart represented the mind and will while the intestines
represented the emotions and feelings. The mind and the
emotions are the two areas where the devil most fiercely
attacks Christians. He tempts us to think wrong thoughts
and feel wrong emotions. Satan wants to cloud our thinking
with false teaching and confuse our emotions with per-
verted morals and loyalties.

To protect ourselves against these attacks of the enemy,
we must put on the breastplate of righteousness. But Satan
tries to convince people that God could not possibly forgive
them for some of the horrible things they have done in the
past. He wants us to believe we are worthless in the sight of
God. *Nothing* could be further from the truth.

The righteousness that protects us from Satan is from
Jesus, not from ourselves. It is His complete purity and
perfection before God. It is the knowledge that we have
been completely forgiven of *all* sin and guilt. We are accepted by God as His friends and, even more importantly, as
His sons and daughters because of our relationship with
Christ.

This is our primary defense against the slanderous
attacks of the evil one. We can live confidently and boldly
without guilt, fear, and hopelessness. Our possession of this
righteousness also brings with it responsibility. God supplies
the standard and the necessary power for right living, but
we must be willing to obey Him and His Word on a daily
basis. Failure to do this ultimately results in defeat in the
spiritual battle.

Do you "go with the flow" on your campus or at your
job? Or do you take a stand for what is right, even when the

wrong is the "socially correct" thing to do? Continue to put the righteousness of Jesus in your life by obeying Him rather than following those around you.

The Bible is filled with many examples of how God rewards for obedience. It's the best defense against the slanderous attacks of the devil.

The Shoes of Peace

Next in the list of the soldier's equipment are the shoes. The Roman legionnaire wore leather half-boots with open toes. They had heavily spiked or studded soles and were tied to the ankles and shins with long straps. These shoes equipped him for lengthy marches and prevented his feet from slipping and sliding, giving him a solid stance.

A Christian soldier without the shoes of peace is almost sure to stumble, fall, and suffer defeat at the hands of the enemy. These shoes function in two ways. First, if we have received the gospel of peace (made a commitment to Jesus Christ), it means we are at complete peace with God. And because we are at peace with God, we can also be at peace with ourselves and others, giving us the firmest foothold possible from which to fight evil. We can stand in confidence, knowing that God loves us and that He is committed to fight for us.

Second, the Christian soldier's shoes indicate a readiness to proclaim the good news of peace with God to others. We need to be prepared to share the message of God's love and forgiveness for sin, whenever and wherever God gives us the opportunity—in our homes, on campus, on the job, in our communities. The devil hates and fears the gospel because he knows it is God's power to rescue people from his rule.

Are you prepared to stand up to the devil? Only experiencing God's peace can give you the firm footing you need.

The Shield of Faith

The shield was an indispensable part of the soldier's equipment. In Paul's day, the shield was oblong and approximately 4.5 feet high and 2.5 feet wide, essentially covering the entire body. It was made of two layers of wood glued together then covered with a layer of cloth and a layer of animal hide and finished with a strip of iron on the top and bottom. The shield was uniquely designed to put out and deflect special arrows used at that time that were dipped in sap, then lit and shot at the enemy.

The shield of faith is essential protection for Christian soldiers, an indispensable addition to the rest of our armor. This shield can deflect the enemy's fiery arrows of false guilt, lust, fear, lies, discouragement, temptation, and rebellion.

Genuine, basic faith takes hold of the promises of God in times of depression and doubt and takes hold of the power of God in times of temptation and trials. This shield of faith is the awesome, total protection that God gives us against Satan's attacks. It is available to us when we choose to place our faith and confidence in God as our protector.

Everyone lives by some kind of faith. We eat food, trusting that it has not been poisoned. We put our faith in cars, buses and planes, believing that they are safe. But faith in God is much more important than the everyday faith we live by. Jesus Christ is incredibly powerful and more dependable than anything we know because He *never* fails.

Be careful of the devil's flaming arrows of temptation to get you to doubt God. You can depend on the Lord to protect you and provide for you.

Helmet of Salvation

The Roman soldier's helmet was usually made of a tough metal—like iron or bronze—and was designed to protect the head from injury. An inside lining made of sponge or felt helped to make the weight of the helmet more bearable. Sometimes there was a hinged visor that added more frontal protection, and these helmets were often decorated with huge plumes. Only an ax or hammer could pierce these heavy helmets. A soldier would never enter battle without it.

While this military helmet was designed to protect the soldier's head, the helmet of salvation is designed to protect the Christian's mind. Satan's attacks are directed at our security and assurance in Christ. He will do everything he can to cause discouragement and doubt by pointing out anything that may be negative in our lives. He wants to throw obstacles in our way, sidetrack us, and make us lose our confidence in God. He wants us to doubt the promises in God's Word.

As you know, the heart of spiritual warfare is really a battle for the mind. God's saving power is the only defense we have against the enemy of our souls. We are to be secure in our salvation and our identity in Christ. We have confidence in the assurance of God's continuing work in our life and in our final "graduation day" to come. God is never going to abandon you, no matter what the situation, and He will always be there for you. His power is available to you to defeat anything the enemy may throw at you.

These first five pieces of armor that God has given us have been primarily defensive weapons. Now the focus changes to equipment used for offensive warfare.

Sword of the Spirit

A battle-ready Roman soldier was always equipped with weapons that enabled him to defend himself as well as to attack his enemy and achieve victory. Many different kinds of weapons were available, including spears and bows and arrows, but perhaps the most powerful weapon of all was his sword. Usually, this was a short, two-edged dagger which allowed the soldier to respond quickly to an attacker. Fighting would involve a close personal encounter—hand-to-hand combat. The sword was both an offensive and defensive weapon.

God has also armed Christians with a powerful sword. The sword the Lord has given us for spiritual warfare is the Word of God—the Bible. God puts this dagger in our hands so we can use it both in resisting temptation (as Jesus did in the wilderness when He quoted Scripture to the devil), and in sharing the good news with others.

Hebrews 4:12 describes the Bible as being sharper than any two-edged sword. It is sharp enough to shred the lies that Satan attempts to throw at us, and it is sharp enough to cut through the defenses of someone without Christ. But only when we know the Bible and understand its relevancy in our lives will we be able to use the sword effectively. In the next chapter, "Choose Your Weapons," we will discuss in greater detail some ideas on how to study and apply the Bible.

When you are faced with questions about your life, where do you turn? The Bible has real answers about relationships, the future, how to get along with others—everything that relates to your life.

Prayer

The apostle Paul concludes the armor of God with the most important piece of equipment in spiritual warfare: prayer. Equipping ourselves with God's armor can only be done through prayer. The Bible and prayer are the two chief weapons that God places in our hands for battle.

God's power is given to Christians by a simple act of trust in Him. This trust is most commonly demonstrated in the act of prayer. We should pray and ask God for strength to do battle as we put on each piece of armor daily in preparation. Our armor is strengthened through consistent prayer as we tap into the awesome power of God. Paul also reminds us to pray for our brothers and sisters in Christ in their struggle against the forces of darkness.

How much time do you spend each day praying? Someone once said that a prayerless Christian is a powerless Christian—and that person was right! Take time to pray.

The armor of God is not optional for Christians. It is essential for victory against the forces of darkness. Each piece was carefully designed by God to serve a specific purpose. When properly "put on" and used, the armor enables us to stand up to the devil.

Because the devil never exercises a "cease-fire" in the battle, we must always be on the alert for attack. That's why it is crucial to put on the full armor of God every day. Take a few minutes briefly each morning to pray about each piece and carefully put them in place in your life.

God has done a fantastic job of providing all the necessary equipment to stand up to the enemy forces in battle. Now it is our responsibility to secure the equipment, get trained in how to use it, and, most importantly, put it on!

Something to Think About

1. What are you trusting God for today in your life that only He can accomplish? Be specific and take time to prayerfully consider this.

2. Read Proverbs 30:5. What does it mean to come to God for protection?

3. What three pieces of armor must we take up (Ephesians 6:16,17)? Why are these pieces so important in standing up to the devil?

4. Read Philippians 4:6,7. What must we do to experience peace in the midst of the devil's attacks?

———————

13

Choose Your Weapons

You are a soldier in a spiritual war. This is not an optional situation for anyone. Like it or not, you're fighting in an intensive, unseen battle. But you do have a couple of choices to make regarding how you function in combat. First, you must decide who your commanding officer is—the devil or Jesus. Who is it that you take your orders from? If you have never opened your heart to Jesus as Savior and Lord, I want you to jump ahead to the next chapter, "Freedom from the Power of Darkness," and seriously consider this commitment. Then once you have settled this all-important decision, return to this chapter.

Second, you must choose your weapons. Will you fight the battle with human weapons of the world or with God-given spiritual weapons? Too many Christians today are being defeated by the enemy because they are not using the right weapons.

Every Christian possesses the equipment necessary to gain victory in the daily struggle against the world, the flesh, and the devil. These crucial weapons are the sword of the spirit (the Word of God) and prayer. Let's take a look at the sword first and see how we can best use this weapon.

161

The Sword

The Holy Spirit is the "in-house" teacher of truth in our hearts. He makes the sword effective in our lives. In the previous chapter I mentioned that a Roman soldier's sword is usually a small, easily handled dagger, used for up-close precision work. The Word of God must also be handled specifically and precisely to be effective in the believer's life.

The problem is that too many students today are not using their swords. Among teenagers surveyed about Bible reading, 61 percent said they did not read the Bible at all in a typical week. Most of the ones who said they did so (16 percent) read it once a week, 7 percent read it two days per week, 6 percent about three days a week, 5 percent from four to six days each week, and 4 percent read it every day.[1] No wonder so many are leading defeated Christian lives. One of the most important weapons we have is not even being used.

Before we look at specific ways to study and use "the sword," let's take time to answer some common questions about this incredible weapon.

How Is the Bible Different?

The Bible is totally different from any other book that has ever been written throughout all of history. Nothing comes close to matching its teaching and its relevancy. It speaks to our immediate social, political, and spiritual needs, even though it is very old.

The Bible is "one-of-a-kind" because of its:

Uniformity. The Bible contains 66 books written over a span of 1,500 years by more than 40 authors from every walk of life, including kings, princes, poets, fishermen, and scholars. It was written at different times, in different places, and in three different languages (Hebrew, Greek, and Aramaic). Yet despite all these differences, the Bible speaks with harmony and continuity from the beginning to the end.

Endurance. The Bible was originally written on material that was perishable. It had to be copied and recopied for hundreds of years before the invention of the printing press, yet it never lost its style or accuracy. Today there is more manuscript evidence for the Bible than for any ten pieces of ancient literature combined.

Over the years the Bible has withstood vicious attacks from enemies bent on destroying it. People have tried to burn it and ban it, but it has survived and even flourished in the midst of these attacks.

Distribution. The Bible has been published in more languages and read by more people than any other book in history. No other book has even come close to the multiplied millions of copies of the Bible that are in print today.

While none of these unique features can prove that the Bible is the Word of God, any book that is this unusual certainly deserves our attention. There must be something different about it.

Can You Trust the Bible?

People today are searching for real answers they can trust, something to help them sort through the confusion. They're looking for a source of authority they can rely on. The Word of God is the only source we can trust for answers about the issues of life.

There's not enough room in a book like this to discuss *every* reason why we can trust the Bible, but I have listed a few of the main reasons below:

- There is more manuscript evidence for the New Testament than for any other ancient document.

- No other religious literature contains the accuracy of fulfilled prophecy that the Bible does. Predictions that were recorded hundreds of years before an event have been fulfilled in minute detail.

- There is cultural, historical, geographical, and archaeological evidence that supports the reliability of the Bible.

- The Bible is inspired by God (God-breathed). The writers were moved by God to record all that He desired. The process of inspiration extends to every word in the Scripture. And because God is perfect and He is the one behind the writings, the Bible is completely truthful in all its parts.

- The Bible is authoritative and effective because it does what it says it will do.

Yet no matter how many good arguments we can gather from personal experience, science, prophecy, or archaeology, we still cannot ultimately prove that the Bible is true. But as Christians we know it is true because of the Holy Spirit. He is the only one who can prove the Bible is true, and He does this as He works in the mind and heart of the Christian in whom He lives.

Why Should I Study the Bible?

We live in a benefit-oriented society where people are constantly asking, "What's in it for me?" They want to know how they are going to benefit from involvement in any variety of activities. This mindset has transferred into the spiritual dimension of life, especially when it comes to spending time studying the Bible.

The benefits to a regular time in God's Word far outweigh any sacrifice of time and energy on our part. Four of the main advantages are found in 2 Timothy 3:16,17:

> All Scripture is God-breathed and is useful for teaching, rebuking, correcting and training in righteousness, so that the man of God may be thoroughly equipped for every good work.

Everything in the Bible is profitable and deserves our attention. When we read God's Word, He is speaking directly to us. Let's look more carefully at the four main advantages mentioned in these two verses from 2 Timothy.

Teaching. The Bible helps to structure our thinking God's way. We need to think correctly so we can live correctly. Someone once said that what you believe is how you will behave.

Rebuking. God tells us when we are out-of-bounds in our life through His Word. The Holy Spirit convicts us of the things that are wrong and need to be changed. The Bible not only tells us what is sin, but also what God desires in our life.

Correcting. The Bible not only tells us when we are out-of-bounds, but it helps to correct the negatives as well. It opens up the doors in our life and enables us to clean out the sin. The Bible helps us to straighten things up and put them back in proper order.

Training in righteousness. The Bible shows us how to live the way we were created to live. It is a handbook filled with positive guidelines on how to get the most out of life. It is the greatest owner's manual ever written, answering the questions we have and guiding us in the decisions we make.

The bottom line is that the Bible helps us to grow in our relationship with God.

But if the Bible is so unique, trustworthy, and valuable, why don't people spend more time reading it on a weekly basis?

We could come up with a number of excuses. Maybe it's because we have become so visually oriented with TV, videos, and computers that the Bible doesn't appeal to us all that much. Or maybe we don't think we have the time. Or the Bible doesn't seem that relevant. Or one of a million other reasons why we don't spend time in God's Word.

Take a minute and check your own study habits:

- How often do you read the Bible?

- When you do read it, how much time do you spend?

- If you don't read it, why not? (Think very specifically.)

I am convinced that the devil will throw any number of obstacles (some will even be good things) in our way to keep us out of God's Word. That's all the more reason to make Bible study a priority and discipline ourselves to make time for it on a consistent basis. Satan recognizes the power of Scripture in our lives, and so should we. Studying God's Word provides the ultimate protection for daily battles against the enemy, the world, and the flesh.

Before we get into some real practical, hands-on ways to get into the Word, let's take a quick look at the other crucial piece of our equipment if we are to experience victory in the daily struggles with enemy forces.

Prayer

Someone once said that Satan trembles when he sees the weakest saint on his knees. As we discussed in the last chapter, there is no doubt that prayer is the most important piece of equipment we have for spiritual warfare. Prayer is more than expressing our thoughts to God or presenting our list of needs to Him. Prayer demonstrates our total dependence on God for help, hope, guidance, and direction in our lives.

People from all walks of life throughout history have come to realize the value and necessity of prayer. President Abraham Lincoln once said, "I have been driven many times to my knees by the overwhelming conviction that I had nowhere else to go. My own wisdom, and that of all about me, seemed insufficient for the day."

Have you reached that place in your life where you realize that prayer is not just the only place you can go but also the *best* place you can go for help? Prayer for the Christian is like spiritual breathing—an absolute necessity for life!

Prayer is probably the most misunderstood and under-used aspect of the Christian life. It's so much more than "Rub-a-dub-dub, bless this grub, God." And it is much more than some meaningless repetition we sometimes get caught up in to fulfill our "spiritual duty." We often fail to realize the significance, power, and privilege of prayer. Imagine the Creator of the universe actually listening to us and responding to our needs. It's awesome!

Like anything else associated with spiritual growth, we must dedicate quality time to prayer. There is a price to pay, but what we stand to gain far outweighs any cost involved. Whatever you have to do with school, relationships, sports, or a job, nothing is more important than developing your spiritual life.

In the rest of this chapter we will look at some practical tips on how to develop a consistent "quiet time" with the Lord.

Getting into the Word and Prayer

This section on the practical "how to's" is not meant to make you feel guilty or overwhelm you with totally unrealistic expectations for getting into the Word and prayer. If you are already spending time alone with God, I hope this section will be an encouragement to you to keep doing what you're doing, and maybe give you some tips on how to enhance and strengthen your Bible study and prayer time.

If this is something you'd like to begin doing, I want to help you understand how you can study the Bible for yourself and begin to develop your prayer life. We'll work at setting some realistic, obtainable goals so you can gradually develop the habit of a daily, consistent time alone with God. But let's be realistic. If you are not doing that already, you can't expect to go from nothing to everything overnight. After all, how do you eat an elephant? One bite at a time! How do you develop a consistent time alone with God? One day at a time!

Here's a simple plan to get you started.

Developing a Time Alone with God

Before you actually start having a regular time alone with God, you need to establish some ground rules.

1. Set a regular time and place. Make an appointment with God and keep it. Don't let anything keep you from that time. I think morning is generally the best time. Time alone with God in the morning helps us prepare to face the challenges of the day. Also, make sure the place you have chosen will be free from distractions.

2. Establish realistic goals for yourself in regard to how often and how long. For example, plan on having a quiet time three days this week. If you end up doing more, terrific! But it's better to start slow and gradually build than to crash and burn the first week.

I'd like to also suggest that you plan for 15 minutes each quiet time. If you want to do more, fantastic! The important thing is to be realistic and work at developing consistency.

3. Have a plan for reading. There are several ways you can develop a plan for studying the Bible, depending on your preference. You can choose to read through a book in the Old or New Testament. For example, you could decide to read a proverb every day or one of the Gospels (Matthew, Mark, Luke, or John). A chapter is always a good way to start, but the issue is not how much you read, but rather that you understand what you've read and apply it to your life.

You could do a word study on something that interests you. Most Bibles have a concordance in the back and with that you can look up words like *love, peace, anger,* or whatever you choose. Make note of what the Bible has to say about that word and how it is used.

A topical study is another way to use your quiet time. The best resource for this is a topical Bible that lists various subjects and where they can be found in the Scriptures.

Or you can do a character study of a particular person in the Bible. There are some fascinating people in Scripture who teach us a lot about life. (There are ideas to help you get started in all these different kinds of study on p. 174.)

Whatever plan you decide to use for reading, remember that a Scripture reference is like an address. It tells you where the verse "lives" in the Bible. For example, the reference "John 3:16." It is read, "John three sixteen." "John" is the name of the book, the fourth book in the New Testament. The "3" refers to the third chapter in the book. And the verse number is "16." It's not too hard—just takes a little practice.

If you're not a big reader or have trouble reading, give thought to getting a copy of the Bible on tape. It's a great way to study the Bible as you spend time alone with God. It also has the advantage of helping you grow as you jog, work out, roller blade, or drive in your car. Most Christian bookstores have several different versions on tape.

4. Have a plan for recording God's truth. As you read the Bible, keep certain questions in mind about the passage:

- What is happening? What is the outcome? What is God's promise for me?

- Who is talking or being talked about? (principal characters)

- Where did this take place? Where have they been? Where are they going?

- When did this happen? (in history or the life of this person)

- Why did this happen? Why was it said?

- How does this apply to me? What do I need to do?

Take time to carefully examine each passage you read in light of these questions. Don't be afraid to underline key verses or circle key words that grab your attention. If you have a question, make a note about it and ask your parents or your youth pastor.

Keeping Track of What You Discover

Once you decide on your plan, you'll find it helpful to have a place to record what you are discovering. Take some time to develop a spiritual journal to keep track of what you are reading, learning, and praying about.

There are sample forms on pages 172 and 173 to get you started. (Feel free to photocopy the forms for your own use.) Following those you will find some ideas for word studies, books, topics, and characters. It's not an exhaustive list, but it does get you started. (There are more ideas in my *Bible Study and Prayer Handbook for Students*. Contact my ministry for additional information.)

We study the Word and spend time praying because we want to grow in our relationship with God. Spending time alone with the Lord helps us to know Him better and to become more like Jesus in the way we live.

Something to Think About

1. What is the best time of day for you to spend time in God's Word and prayer? Make an appointment with God by setting a specific time now.

2. Where would be the best place in your house to get alone with God? Make sure that you will not be disturbed by a pet, family member, the TV, etc.

3. What is your initial goal for the number of days you will spend time in the Word and prayer? Be realistic and specific.

4. What type of plan are you going to follow for studying the Bible? Be sure to start with something that interests you. It will help you to stay motivated.

5. What is the biggest challenge or concern you are facing in your life right now? Spend the next few minutes in prayer, asking for God's guidance and help for the situation. Make sure you list this prayer request on the prayer form in this chapter.

Bible Study Chart

Date: Bible book:

Chapter: Verses:

Main theme or thought (one sentence):

Key verse (where appropriate):

Summary (In your own words summarize what the author is saying in a paragraph.):

Application (How does this apply to me?):

Action (What do I need to do? When, where, and with whom?):

God's promise (where appropriate):

Prayer Requests

What am I asking God to do, answer, or provide?

Date   **Request**   **Date Answered**

Ideas to Help Get You Started

Word Studies

- *Love:* Matthew 5:43; 22:37; Luke 6:35; John 15:13; 1 Corinthians 13; Ephesians 2:4,5.
- *Evil:* Genesis 2:9; Judges 3:7; Job 1:8; Psalm 34:14; Proverbs 8:13.

Book Studies

- Proverbs
- Mark
- James

Topical Studies

- *Loneliness:* 1 Kings 18 and 19.
- *Growth and Maturity:* Romans 5:1-11; 6:1-14.

Character Studies

- *Ruth:* Read the book of Ruth.
- *Jonah:* Read the book of Jonah.

14

Freedom from the Power of Darkness

Dear Steve,

Howz everything going? I heard you speak last month and I just want to thank you. I had been involved in the occult for over a year. I was a third-rank leader, and I helped lead some of the rituals that we went through.

Last year I had "rededicated" my life to Christ, but only as a joke. I felt that if God really loved me more than Satan, He would have given me the life I needed or wanted. Our group used to go through many satanic rituals and other things to worship the devil. We would do anything for Satan.

After listening to you speak, I realized that God was real and that Satan was not the person I should be worshipping. I gave my life to Christ at your meeting, and I'm glad I did. When I returned home, I found out that one of the guys under my leadership had been picked up by the police. He had mentioned my name along with many other names of the people in our group. He is now being tried for vandalism and murder.

God used this situation to allow me to drop out of the occult in order to stay out of juvenile hall.

I realize now that I had been missing out on God's love because I had turned to Satan out of bitterness for the world. I am now trying to spread God's love instead of Satan's lies. My story may not seem to be the greatest testimony, but I feel that if God can help me to get out of the occult, then maybe my story can help others realize that God is more powerful than Satan and can help anybody out of any situation. And I've also learned that no matter what you've done, God will forgive you and help you to receive His love and eternal life.

Love always,
Tiffany

As Tiffany found out, there is hope, power, and victory to be found in the person of Jesus Christ. Satan is cruel, clever, and powerful. His power goes way beyond our human, natural power. If you're not plugged into the power of God, if you don't know Christ, then you can't hope to resist the devil and the power of evil around you.

Hanging around a church doesn't make you a Christian. Some students live a totally worldly life all week long and then like to show up at the youth group meeting on Sunday or Wednesday and play the game. Have you checked out your motives? Are you really committed to God? Do you really know Christ?

Choosing to Follow Jesus

The most important thing you can do in life is to make a sincere commitment to follow Jesus as Savior and Lord, and then to grow in this very special relationship with the living God. Jesus is standing before you today with His arms open wide saying, "Trust Me. Believe in Me. I love you and want to have a personal relationship with you." Jesus is not only our defender, but He died on a cross to make a new and exciting life possible for us as well.

The dark occultic world of Satan may have a certain appeal—temporarily—but God has a billion times more to offer in a satisfying and purposeful relationship with Him. But we must *choose* to follow Jesus. No one can make this decision for us, and going to church isn't enough.

If you have not yet decided to follow Jesus, I want to give you an opportunity to do so now. Freedom from the power of darkness begins when you surrender your life to Jesus. It is the truth that sets you free. Jesus said in John 14:6, "I am the way and the truth and the life. No one comes to the Father except through me."

If you want to establish the most important relationship of your life by opening your heart to Christ, here are the steps to follow:

1. Admit that you are a sinner and have a need for a relationship with God.

   All of us have sinned and fallen short of God's glory (Romans 3:23 CEV).

2. Be willing to repent (turn away from your sin) and start living your life depending on God.

   That if you confess with your mouth, "Jesus is Lord," and believe in your heart that God raised him from the dead, you will be saved (Romans 10:9).

3. Believe that Jesus died for you on the cross and after three days rose from the grave.

> But God showed how much he loved us by having Christ die for us, even though we were sinful (Romans 5:8 CEV).

4. By a simple act of faith, through prayer, invite Jesus to come in and control your life through the Holy Spirit.

> Here I am! I stand at the door and knock. If anyone hears my voice and opens the door, I will come in and eat with him, and he with me (Revelation 3:20).

Here's a prayer you can use to make this commitment:

Dear Lord Jesus,

I admit that I am a sinner and need Your forgiveness. I believe that You died for my sins. I want to turn away from my sins and start following You. I now invite You to come into my heart and life. I want to trust You as my Savior and follow You as the Lord of my life.

I pray this in Jesus' name. Amen.

The Bible teaches that if we sincerely ask Jesus Christ to come into our lives, He will: "Everyone who calls on the name of the Lord will be saved" (Romans 10:13). Jesus said, "I give them eternal life, and they shall never perish; no one can snatch them out of my hand" (John 10:28). You are safe and secure in Christ.

If you do pray to receive Christ as your Savior and Lord,

write me at the address in the back of the book. I'd like to send you some things to help you get started in this exciting new relationship. Why don't you tell someone else about this decision you have made? And if you aren't already, get involved in a good local church.

You're Already a Christian, But...

What do you do when you've made a commitment to follow Jesus and still don't seem to be experiencing freedom? You try and try and try, but your Christian life just isn't working. It's possible that somehow the enemy has gained a foothold in your life. Your eternal relationship with God isn't at stake, but you need to take responsibility for taking a stand against the enemy's lies. You must choose truth in the battle for your mind and emotions. In this chapter we'll walk through seven steps that will take you to the total freedom and victory that Jesus made possible through His death on the cross.

This is something you must *choose* to do, just like following Jesus. While no one can do it for you, I do want to encourage you to ask a mature Christian to be with you when you walk through these steps. (This could be a close friend, parent, youth pastor, etc.) You can find freedom in Christ if you choose to believe, confess, forgive, renounce, and forsake what is keeping you from victory in your daily life.

Steps to Freedom in Christ[1]

These seven steps are designed to help you experience the liberty and success that God has planned for you in your daily life. As you walk through them, remember that the battle is ultimately for your mind. So as you go through these steps, you may struggle with strange thoughts like, "There's no way this is going to work for me," "I'm no good," or "Don't worry about this now. There's plenty of time to do this later." Those are lies straight from the lips of the devil. They're meant to confuse and mislead you.

If you are working through these steps alone, just keep moving ahead and don't pay any attention to Satan's lies. If another Christian is helping you, share your thoughts and ask him or her to pray for you. Remember, Satan's power is in the lie. Once you choose the truth, the devil's power is broken.

As you take each step, it is very important that you submit to God in your heart and then resist the devil by reading out loud each prayer and statement. Satan can't read your mind, so your stand against him needs to be verbalized.

Now you're ready to begin. Start by sincerely praying this prayer out loud:

> Dear Heavenly Father,
>
> I acknowledge Your presence in this room and in my life. You are the only all-powerful, all-knowing, and ever-present living God. I need You because I know that I can do nothing without Jesus. I believe the Bible because it tells me what is really true. I refuse to believe the lies of the enemy. I claim the truth that all authority in heaven and on earth has been given to the resurrected Christ. Please fill me with Your Holy Spirit and protect my mind and emotions. I ask for Your complete protection and guidance to live the truth in my life.
>
> I pray this in Jesus' name. Amen.

If someone else is walking through these steps with you, ask him or her to declare the following for you, or proclaim it out loud for yourself:

> Lord Jesus Christ, we ask by the authority and power of Your name that You command Satan and all evil spirits to let go of (your name) in order that (your name) can be free to know and choose to do the will of God. Lord Jesus, we also ask that You bind and gag to silence every enemy. We believe that Satan and all of his evil workers cannot inflict any pain or hinder God's will from being done today in (your name).

You may experience demonic interference during the early stages of these steps to freedom. Remember that prayer is our ultimate weapon against such attacks. You have sufficient authority and power in Christ to help you to gain your freedom. Even though you may struggle through these steps, you will learn a valuable lesson in the process: You can win a spiritual battle whenever you are under attack as long as you resist Satan and call upon the Lord for help.

Throughout the following steps you will be asked to confess and renounce various things in prayer. To *confess* means to admit openly that you have done something and agree with God that it is wrong. To *renounce* is to turn your back on any past or present activity that is wrong by God's standards and decide not to do it again.

Step 1: Standing Up to Counterfeits

The first step to freedom is to confess and renounce any present or past involvement with any satanic or occultic practices or false religions. You must turn your back on any group or activity that tries to direct your life through any source other than the Bible, denies Jesus Christ, or requires secret initiations, pacts, or ceremonies. If you are a Christian, you have no business participating in a group that is not completely open about who they are and what they do (1 John 1:5-7).

You must not only reject the lies of the devil, but you must also choose to live the truth. There is no neutral ground when it comes to Jesus. You are either for Him or against Him (Luke 11:23). Many other religions and groups may mention Jesus, but they present Him as something less than who He really is in the Bible. They fail to acknowledge Him as the Son of God.

In order to help you identify any activities or practices of darkness that you may have been involved in, take some time to fill out the "Spiritual Counterfeit Checklist" (p. 183). Be sure to add anything that you may have been involved in that is missing from the list. Even if you just watched something at a party or were "innocently" involved in something, renounce it so Satan can't have any footholds in your life.

Don't be surprised if you sense some resistance as you walk through this step. The devil will do anything possible to keep you from being free in Christ.

Pray the following out loud as you go through this step:

Dear Heavenly Father,

I ask You to help me remember anything that I have done or that someone has done to me that is spiritually wrong. Show me any satanic or occultic practices that I may have been involved in, even if I thought it was innocent. I want to experience Your freedom and do Your will.

I ask this in Jesus' name. Amen.

Spiritual Counterfeit Checklist

Read over the following list. Place a check beside any activity you participated in either voluntarily or involuntarily.

Occult

_____ Astral projection

_____ Bloody Mary

_____ Using spells or curses

_____ Spirit guides

_____ Astrology/horoscopes

_____ Magic eight ball

_____ Visualization/guided imagery

_____ Palm reading

_____ Tarot cards

_____ Sorcery

_____ Crystals, good luck charms or idols

_____ Black or white magic

_____ Ouija board

_____ Table lifting or body lifting

_____ Automatic writing

_____ Fortune-telling

_____ Using spells or curses

_____ Rituals/sacrifices

_____ Blood pacts or cutting yourself in a destructive way

_____ Hypnosis

_____ Witchcraft

_____ Seances

_____ Dungeons and Dragons (or other FRPs)

_____ Other experiences

Cults

_____ Mormonism

_____ Christian Science

_____ Jehovah's Witnesses

_____ Wicca

_____ Scientology

_____ New Age (including medicine)

_____ Others:

Other Religions

_____ Zen Buddhism

_____ Islam

_____ Voodoo

_____ Yoga

_____ Hinduism

_____ Santeria

_____ Transcendental Meditation

_____ Others:

Write down the titles of any satanic or occultic movies, music, books, magazines, comic books, TV programs, computer, video, or board games that you may have been involved in:

Movies—

Music—

Books, magazines, comic books—

TV programs—

Computer, video, or board games—

Finally, consider the following questions:

1. Have you ever felt, seen, or heard a spiritual presence in your room?

2. Have you had an imaginary friend or inner child who you talk to?

3. Have you ever heard voices in your head or had repeating thoughts like, "I'm worthless," or "I'm a loser," etc., almost as if there were a conversation going on in your head?

4. Have you ever consulted a psychic, medium, spiritist, or channeler?

5. Have you ever had any very unusual spiritual experiences that have frightened you (telepathy, trance, etc.)?

6. Have you ever been involved in any form of satanic worship or been at a concert where the devil was being exalted?

After you are sure your list is complete, use the following prayer to confess and renounce each involvement or activity. Pray out loud and repeat the prayer separately for each item on your list.

Dear Lord,

> I confess that I _____. I ask
> Your forgiveness, and I renounce _____
> as a spiritual counterfeit to true Christianity.

Step 2: Standing Up to Deception

The devil has done a masterful job at confusing people about truth. More than 70 percent of those surveyed under the age of 25 said they do not believe in absolute truth.[2] Satan knows that the truth exposes his deception and sets us free. God wants us to live the truth so we can become the people He designed us to be. The source of absolute truth that brings freedom is God's Word, the Bible. But in order to live the truth, we must get rid of anything false in our lives and speak the truth in love (Ephesians 4:15,25).

To begin this important step, read the following prayer out loud:

> Dear Heavenly Father,
>
> I know that You want the truth from me and that I must be honest with You. I recognize that choosing to believe Your truth will set me free. I have been fooled by Satan, the father of lies, and I have fooled myself. I thought I could hide it from You, but You see everything and still love me. I pray in the name of the Lord Jesus Christ, asking You to rebuke all of Satan's demons through the power of Your resurrected Son, Jesus. I have asked Jesus into my life, and I know that I am Your child. Lord, I also ask You to command all evil spirits to stop harassing me. And I ask the Holy Spirit to lead me into all

truth. Please look deep inside me and know my
heart. Show me if there is anything in me that I
am trying to hide, because I want to be free.
I ask all this in Jesus' name. Amen.

I would like you to take some time now to think of any
deceptive lies Satan has tempted you with. Maybe you've
been listening to false teaching or deceiving yourself. Have
you been trying to escape or hide behind excuses to justify
your actions? God has forgiven you and you are alive in
Christ. You don't have to live a lie or try to escape anymore.
Think about the following questions as you evaluate your
life:

1. Have you been hearing God's Word and not doing it?

2. Have you been trying to be something or someone
   you're really not?

3. Have you been sexually active in hopes of keeping a
   relationship together?

4. Do you think you can escape the consequences of your
   choices?

5. Do you think you have no sin?

6. Have you believed you can hang around with the wrong
   crowd and it won't have any effect on you?

7. Have you tried to escape the real world through drugs or
   alcohol?

8. Do you blame others or take out your frustrations on
   them?

9. Have you been lying so much that you are starting to
   believe the lies yourself?

10. Are you constantly trying to find an excuse to justify your actions?

Now spend some time in prayer for the things that have been true in your life. Pray out loud:

Dear Lord,

I acknowledge that I have been deceived in the way of _____. Please forgive me for what I've done. Help me to know and follow Your truth.

Start trusting God to help you stop living the lies of your past. Choose to put your faith in the Lord and His Word. Remember, it's what or who we believe in that's important. Declare what you believe based on the truth of God's Word, the Bible. Read the following "Declaration of Truth" out loud. If necessary, read it every day to renew your mind.

Declaration of Truth

1. I believe that there is only one true God who is the Father, the Son, and the Holy Spirit. I believe that He made all things and holds all things together. He is the one who is worthy of all honor, praise, and glory.

2. I believe that Jesus Christ is the Son of God, and that on the cross He defeated Satan and all his demons.

3. I believe that God loves me so much that He gave His own Son to die on the cross so I could be forgiven for all my sins. Jesus delivered me from the powers of darkness

because He loves me, not because of how good or bad I am or anything I could have done.

4. I choose to believe that I am spiritually strong because the Lord Jesus is my strength. I have the authority to stand against the devil because I am God's child. In order to stay strong, I am going to obey God, believe His Word, and put on the full armor of God.

5. I believe that I cannot win any spiritual battles without Jesus, so I choose to totally depend on Him. Jesus is my Lord and Savior. I will resist the devil and any counterfeits that he may choose to tempt me with so that he will flee from me.

6. I believe that only the truth will set me free. If Satan tries to put bad thoughts into my mind, I will not pay attention to them. I will no longer listen to Satan's lies, and I will not do what he wants me to do. Rather, I will stand against the devil and his schemes. I choose to believe that the Bible is true, and I choose to speak the truth in love.

7. I choose to use my body to do only good things, as a holy and living sacrifice to God. I will not give Satan a foothold in my life by using my body in the wrong way. I believe that what God wants me to do is the best thing for me, so I choose to do God's will.

8. I ask my Heavenly Father to fill me with His Holy Spirit, to guide me into all truth, and to give me the power to live a victorious Christian life. I love the Lord my God with all my heart, soul, and mind.

Special help for those struggling with eating disorders. Young people with eating disorders (such as anorexia and bulimia) are often driven by Satan's lies to defecate, vomit, or cut themselves. Many believe they are purging themselves of evil. Thoughts of suicide can be common.

The typical young person with an eating disorder is a female who is physically attractive. From the time she was very young she received strokes for her physical appearance. She became so body-conscious that her mind was fertile ground for the enemy's lies. Satan was able to convince her that her worth was based on physical appearance. Instead of controlling her body, she is now being controlled by her body (1 Corinthians 9:27). To be free, she needs to renounce her false identity based on her physical appearance and choose to find her identity in Christ.

If you are suffering from an eating disorder, renounce your behavior out loud as follows:

Kingdom of Darkness	Kingdom of Light
I renounce vomiting to purge myself of evil and reject the lie that my self-worth is based on my physical appearance.	I announce that all food created by God is good and that nothing is to be rejected by those who know the truth.
I renounce taking laxatives and defecating to purge myself of evil.	I announce that it is not what enters my mouth that defiles me but what comes from the heart.
I renounce cutting myself to purge myself of evil.	I announce that only the blood of Jesus can cleanse me.

Step 3: Standing Up to Bitterness

One of the most frequent ways that the devil gains a

foothold in the life of a Christian is through unforgiveness. If you refuse to forgive those who offend or hurt you, you become an easy target for the enemy. God wants us to forgive others so Satan can't take advantage of us (2 Corinthians 2:10,11). Because God has forgiven us, He wants us to forgive others in the same way (Ephesians 4:31,32).

As you read the following prayer out loud, ask God to bring to your mind those who you need to forgive:

> Dear Heavenly Father,
>
> Thank You for Your kindness, patience, and love toward me. I know that I have not been completely kind, patient, and loving toward others, especially those who have hurt me. I've been bitter and resentful. I ask You to bring to my memory all the people who have hurt me that I need to forgive. And I ask You to heal me from all my hurts.
>
> I pray this in the powerful name of Jesus. Amen.

Get out a blank sheet of paper and make a list of everyone who has hurt you in some way. Don't be surprised at some of the names that pop up, like your parents or yourself. If you're angry with someone, you need to forgive him or her. To forgive someone means you are "letting go" of that hurt. You are not expecting any payment for what this person has done, neither are you going to seek revenge.

To forgive someone does not mean you will forget what happened. Instead it means you are letting go so you can move on with your life. And it means you are leaving it up to God to deal with that person. Forgiveness is a choice we must make, even when it seems like an impossibility. And sometimes the ones who are hardest to forgive are those closest to us.

Forgiving those who hurt us is God's way of healing us. Forgiveness is believing that God will deal with the other person in the right way, at the proper time, and heal you from the pain he or she caused you. Being bitter will not solve anything, and it only hurts. It becomes like a cancer to our spiritual life, slowly eating away at us. That's why it is so important to learn to forgive from the heart.

To forgive others from the heart, you must admit your hurt and hatred instead of trying to keep it deep inside. Let God help you face the hurt honestly and openly. Because God has already forgiven everyone on your list, He can help you do the same.

For each person on your list, read the following prayer out loud:

Dear Lord,

I forgive (name) for (specifically name all the hurts or offenses that come to your mind).

I encourage you to keep praying about each person on your list until all the pain has surfaced and been dealt with. Make sure you take whatever time is necessary. Once you have properly forgiven everyone on your list, fold the piece of paper in half and destroy it as a symbol of your desire to let it go. This can be done by ripping the paper up or even throwing it into a fireplace. Destroy it in such a way so you can't go back and dig up the old hurts again.

Step 4: Standing Up to Rebellion

It's easy to develop an "attitude" because of the rebellious times in which we live. Many students today don't respect or submit to the authorities God has placed in their lives. Unfortunately, Christians are no exception. But rebelling against parents, God, and other authority figures is one more way the devil can gain a foothold in our lives. So we must learn to take a stand against it.

The Bible says we have two responsibilities toward the human authorities God has placed in our lives: Submit to them and pray for them. The only time God allows us to disobey them is when they ask us to do something that is morally and spiritually wrong before Him. Unfortunately, there are times when people abuse the authority they have been given, causing a great deal of pain. In times like this, we need to seek protection. And when we are asked to violate God's laws by someone in a position of authority, we need to always obey God, not man.

Take a quick look at the following verses to learn how God wants us to respond to authority:

Government

> Obey the rulers who have authority over you. Only God can give authority to anyone, and he puts these rulers in their places of power. People who oppose the authorities are opposing what God has done, and they will be punished (Romans 13:1,2 CEV).

Parents

> Children, you belong to the Lord, and you do the right thing when you obey your parents. The first commandment with a promise says, "Obey your father and mother, and you will have a long and happy life" (Ephesians 6:1-3 CEV).

Employer

Servants, you must obey your masters and always show respect to them. Do this, not only to those who are kind and thoughtful, but also to those who are cruel. God will bless you, even if others treat you unfairly for being loyal to Him (1 Peter 2:18,19 CEV).

Church Leaders

Obey your leaders and do what they say. They are watching over you, and they must answer to God. So don't make them sad as they do their work. Make them happy. Otherwise, they won't be able to help you at all (Hebrews 13:17 CEV).

Now pray the following prayer out loud:

Dear Heavenly Father,

You have said in the Bible that rebellion is as bad as witchcraft and disobedience is like honoring other gods. I know that I have disobeyed You and rebelled in my heart against You and others that You have put in authority in my life. I ask for Your forgiveness for my rebellion. Please reveal to me all ways that I have been rebellious to You. By the shed blood of the Lord Jesus Christ, I resist all evil spirits who took advantage of my rebellion. Please help me to have a submissive attitude and a servant's heart.

I ask this in the name of the Lord Jesus Christ. Amen.

As we submit to the authorities God has placed in our lives, we are choosing to stand against the devil and trusting God for His protection and blessing. Demonstrate your trust in God to work in the authorities He has placed in your life by praying:

> Father,
>
> I agree that I have been rebellious toward _____. Please forgive me for my rebellion and help me to be obedient to Your Word and will for my life.
> In Jesus' precious name I pray. Amen.

It's a battle for the mind, so be careful of what you might be putting in it that has themes of violence and rebellion.

Step 5: Standing Up to Pride

Pride has destroyed a lot of people. It's an attitude that is found throughout our society. It says, "I can do all things through myself," or "Unleash the power within you." These attitudes of pride are the very core of what sin is: living independent of God. Once again, Satan has put us on a path that leads to destruction by deceiving us into believing we don't need God.

The Bible says that pride comes before destruction (Proverbs 16:18). Numerous times throughout the Bible, we read of the spiritual problems that come as a result of pride (see James 4:6-10 and 1 Peter 5:1-10 to start with). Instead of being filled with pride, we are to humble ourselves before the Lord (James 4:10). And rather than just looking out for our own selfish interests, we are to serve one another in love (Galatians 5:13).

Use the following prayer to confess and renounce an attitude of pride:

> Dear Father in Heaven,
>
> I humble myself before You as I confess to You an attitude of pride. I admit that I have been thinking mainly of myself and not of others. I have believed that I am the only one who cares about me, so I have to take care of myself. I have turned away from You and not let You love me or provide for me. I am tired of living for myself and by myself. I renounce my pride and ask You to fill me with Your Spirit so I can do Your will. I give my heart to You and stand against all the prideful ways that Satan attacks me. I ask You to show me how to live for others. I now choose to make others more important than myself and to make You the most important of all.
>
> I ask this all in the name of my Lord and Savior Jesus Christ. Amen.

Now take some time and allow God to show you any specific areas in your life where pride has been a problem.

Attitude Check for Pride

1. Do you think of yourself as better than others?

2. Do you attempt to satisfy yourself, no matter what the cost?

3. Do you want people to think you have all the answers?

4. Do you find yourself wearing masks to hide who you really are?

5. Are you hard to get along with and do you argue a lot?

6. Do you try to make people think you are humble?

7. Are you always trying to please other people rather than God?

8. Do you often try to control others?

9. Do you often brag about yourself and what you have accomplished?

10. Would others say you have an ego problem?

11. Do you find it difficult to rely on God?

12. Are you more concerned about doing your will rather than God's?

13. Are you so concerned about your opinion being right that you feel everyone else is wrong?

For each of the questions that you answered yes to, pray the following prayer out loud:

Dear Lord,

I agree with You that I have been prideful in the area of _____. Please forgive me for my pride and help me to humble myself. I want to put all my confidence in You.

In Jesus' name I pray. Amen.

If pride has been a real struggle in your life, you may want to consider committing the following verses to memory: Psalm 25:9; Isaiah 66:2; Ephesians 4:2; James 4:10; 1 Peter 5:6.

Step 6: Standing Up to Bad Habits

Sometimes we find ourselves caught up in doing the same old sin day in and day out. We know what we are doing is wrong, but it has become a bad habit for us. Oftentimes the only way to be truly free from sinful habits is to find someone who will not only pray specially for you, but will also keep you accountable. James 5:16 puts it this way: "Therefore confess your sins to each other and pray for each other so that you may be healed. The prayer of a righteous man is powerful and effective." Find someone you respect who is spiritually mature and ask him or her to pray for you and to hold you accountable.

Or maybe what you need to do is get serious about stopping the habitual sin and confess it on the basis of 1 John 1:9: "If we confess our sins, he is faithful and just and will forgive us our sins and purify us from all unrighteousness." There is a tremendous sense of freedom that comes from standing up to a bad habit. Before you ask God to help you deal with these issues, pray the following prayer:

> Dear Heavenly Father,
>
> I admit that I have been struggling with sins that have become habits for me. Please cleanse me and free me from the bondage I am now in. Reveal to me any and all bad habits that need to be broken.
>
> I pray this in the powerful name of Jesus. Amen.

In Galatians 5:16-21, God gives us a starting point to examine our lives for sins that have become habits. Let's take a look:

If you are guided by the Spirit, you won't obey your selfish desires. The Spirit and your desires are enemies of each other. They are always fighting each other and keeping you from doing what you feel you should. But if you obey the Spirit, the law of Moses has no control over you.

People's desires make them give in to immoral ways, filthy thoughts, and shameful deeds. They worship idols, practice witchcraft, hate others, and are hard to get along with. People become jealous, angry, and selfish. They not only argue and cause trouble, but they are envious. They get drunk, carry on at wild parties, and do other evil things as well. I told you before and I am telling you again: No one who does these things will share in the blessings of God's kingdom (CEV).

Here's a list of some things that you may need to confess and renounce in securing your freedom:

- Sexual sins (pornography, masturbation, promiscuity, petting, homosexuality)

- Sexual sins that were done to you against your will (rape, incest, molestation). While there is nothing you need to ask forgiveness for, you will want to renounce these acts in your life.

- Abortion

- Suicidal tendencies

- Substance abuse (tobacco, prescription and street drugs, alcohol and food)

Read the following prayer aloud:

> Dear Heavenly Father,
>
> I confess to You that I have willfully and sometimes habitually sinned against You. Please forgive me for _____ and give me the power to be freed from this bondage. I now take a stand against the devil and his lies. I choose to live the right kind of life by following the standards in Your Word so I can be free.
> In Jesus' name I pray. Amen.

Because of the seriousness of some of these habitual or special sins, I encourage you to seek some help and encouragement from a mature Christian. And remember, if you have confessed a sin and are still feeling guilty, you may be listening to a false accusation from the enemy. The Holy Spirit does convict us of sin in our lives, but God will never make us feel guilty for something that has already been dealt with.

Step 7: Standing Up to the Sins of Ancestors

The last step to freedom, as you stand up to the devil, is to turn your back on the sins of your ancestors (parents, grandparents, great-grandparents, etc.).

When God gave the Ten Commandments in the Old Testament, He said,

> You shall not make yourselves any idols: any images resembling animals, birds, or fish. You must never bow to an image or worship it in any way; for I, the Lord your God, am very possessive. I will not share your affection with any

other god! And when I punish people for their sins, the punishment continues upon the children, grandchildren, and great-grandchildren of those who hate me; but I lavish my love upon thousands of those who love me and obey my commandments (Exodus 20:4-6 TLB).

While we are not guilty of these sins, the devil may use them to gain a foothold in our families. It is our responsibility to renounce any of the sins of our ancestors and to claim our freedom in Christ.

Pray the following prayer out loud to renounce all known or unknown sins of your relatives:

Dear Heavenly Father,

I come to You as Your child, bought by the blood of the Lord Jesus Christ. I have been set free from the power of darkness, and I am now in the Kingdom of God. I am spiritually alive in Christ and united with Him in the spiritual world. Jesus has broken all ties with and workings of Satan that were passed on to me from my ancestors. I therefore turn my back on and reject all the sins of my ancestors.

Because I am owned by Jesus, I reject any and all ways Satan may claim ownership of Me. I announce to all the forces of evil that I am forever and completely committed and signed over to the Lord Jesus Christ. By Your authority and power, Jesus, I ask You to command every evil spirit that is familiar with my family and every enemy of Yours around me to leave me forever. I now ask You, Heavenly Father, to fill me with Your Holy Spirit. I present my body to You as a living sacrifice so people will know that You live in me.

All this I do in the name of the Lord Jesus Christ. Amen.

Now What?

We've covered a lot of important territory in this chapter.

As you think about some of the major spiritual house-cleaning you've done in your life, be aware of the devil's continued attempts to try to gain footholds in your life. He is relentless in his schemes to influence your thinking. The spiritual war will never be over until we go to be with Jesus or until He comes back for the second time.

Our freedom in Christ is eternally secure, but it needs to be maintained on a daily basis. This means that you must keep up your relationship with Jesus. If you find yourself slipping or falling in your spiritual life, get back to the basics. Keep short accounts with God in relation to your sin, and make sure you're spending quality time in the Word and prayer. Stay involved in your church youth group, and double-check to make sure that you have your spiritual armor on.

Jesus has the power and authority to boot the enemy and his forces of darkness out of our lives. But it is our responsibility not to open the door and let the devil back in.

The Lord has promised to never leave us or turn His back on us (Hebrews 13:5). So stand up to the devil, stay away from the darkness, and turn toward the light of the ultimate winner—Jesus Christ!

Something to Think About

1. What does the phrase "freedom in Christ" mean to you?

2. Are there any steps that you are unsure of or that you need to review again? If yes, take some time right now and repeat the step.

3. What steps had the greatest impact on you? Why?

4. Why is it so important to maintain a right relationship with God?

15

Candle in the Dark

Brenda came to me out of concern for a friend. She explained how one of her girlfriends seemed to be totally consumed by the occult and Satan worship. "She doesn't see the danger or even how much her involvement in this darkness is changing her," Brenda said. "I want to help her so badly, but I don't know what to do. Where do I start?"

What can we do to help those we care about "come out of the darkness and into the light"?

God has given us an awesome privilege to be soldiers, under His command, deployed in a massive hostage rescue operation. He has made us light so we might bring others to Jesus (Acts 13:47).

All around us are friends, family members, neighbors, and people at school who are living in darkness. The devil has done a masterful job at getting them to believe his lies. They have no sense of purpose or direction in life because they've never made a decision to follow Jesus as Lord.

And just like Brenda's friend, some people we care about are actually playing with fire and don't recognize the danger of their dabbling in the darkness. How can we recognize if a friend is playing in the devil's playground? Here are some warning signs to look for:

1. *Withdrawal from routine activities.* Beware of un-usual seclusion and secrecy by your friend.

2. *Obsession with death and suicide.* Pay attention to the music your friend is listening to and the videos he or she is watching, especially those that may have occultic themes. Also check any doodles or scribbles on a notebook or book cover with these themes.

3. *Obsession with black.* Your friend could demonstrate this obsession by dyeing his or her hair black, wear-ing dark makeup to an extreme, or dressing totally in black all the time. But be careful not to overreact because black is a very fashionable color today.

4. *Fixation with satanic/occultic symbols.* These sym-bols can be found on a variety of items, including jewelry, clothing, CD covers, comic books, games, etc. Many of these symbols are explained in the appendixes of this book.

5. *Possession of "how to" satanic literature.* These could include a copy of the *Satanic Bible*, books like *Mag-ick* by Alister Crowley, manuals on how to cast spells, etc.

6. *Excessive fear or anxiety.* If your friend exhibits unusual preoccupation and paranoia about current events in the world situation, then you have cause for concern.

7. *Fascination with or possession of knives.* Ceremonial knives of various sizes and shapes are used in satanic rituals, black masses, and sacrifices. It is usually

pretty obvious if your friend's interest is more than just an innocent collection.

8. *Cuts, scratches, burns, and tattoos.* Look for scars or tattoos in the shape of satanic symbols on parts of the body.

9. *Books and journals.* Watch for diaries, drawings, poetry, books, etc. that focus on death, the occult, Satan worship, black magic, reincarnation, or witchcraft. Anything written in blood, backward script, homemade alphabet, or secret code could be connected to the occult.

10. *Satanic altars.* They can be simple or extremely elaborate, and located in a bedroom closet, basement, garage, or attic. Very often they are illuminated by red, black, or white candles. They can be decorated with ritual knives and even animal bones.

To rescue someone from the mine field of the devil's playground, we must first fully understand the level of commitment and preparation that must be in place in our own lives. Like all good soldiers, we must be prepared for battle. In previous chapters we have learned about the equipment God has provided for us. Now let's look at how we can practically use these weapons to make a difference in our world.

How to Be God's Candle

If you want to be used by God as a "candle" in your home, at work, in the neighborhood, or on your campus, take time to evaluate your own life in comparison to each of these "how to" steps.

Stay Close to Jesus

We are secure in Christ and we belong to Him. There is nothing we can do to help ourselves or others in the spiritual battle apart from Jesus. He is our protection, our strength, our defender, and our greatest resource as we face the powers of darkness.

The devil will attempt to make you think you can fight the spiritual battle on your own strength, but keep your heart and mind centered on God's Word. Continue to develop an intimate relationship with the Lord Jesus as you spend time in prayer and the Word. His absolute truth will give you the ability to withstand the deceptive attacks of the enemy.

Be careful of the "demon-buster complex." God has not called us to "kick the devil in the rump." Nor has He called us to go on some sort of "search and destroy" mission to flush out the enemy from the depths of the shadows. Numerous times in His Word the Lord reminds us to stand firm against the devil and he will flee from us. Don't go "gunning" for trouble. Rather, when the attack comes, rely on the strength of the Lord. He will give victory. Stay as close to Jesus as you possibly can on a daily basis.

Don't Be Afraid

Beware of Satan's use of fear to sidetrack you from being a godly influence in your world. A well-meaning missionary called while I was writing this book to warn me about completing the project. Two of the members of our team had just been killed by a drunk driver in a tragic car accident. This missionary said my two friends died because I was writing a book about the devil. "You'd better quit working on this book before the devil kills you, too," he said. "Call the publisher and tell them you want out immediately."

Had I followed his advice, I would have given in to the devil's fear tactic—and that has no place in my life. If we run in the face of the enemy's attacks, we are denying the power of God. Satan's power is limited; God's power is unlimited. We must find a balance between giving Satan more power than what he has and not respecting the power that he actually does possess. While we are facing a fierce opponent, the Bible reminds us that God is greater and will keep us from all evil if we trust Him.

We should never run foolishly into the enemy's camp without being fully prepared. But neither should we run in fear of what Satan might do to us. God is in control, and Satan was mortally wounded by Jesus on the cross. We are on the winning side.

Check and Recheck Your Spiritual Armor

No soldier in his right mind would go off to war without the proper equipment. As Christian soldiers in a spiritual battle, we are no different. The armor God has given us is absolutely critical. Make it a practice each day to check and recheck your "spiritual gear." Make sure that to the best of your knowledge everything is securely in place. You can do this through prayer. Open up your Bible to Ephesians 6:13-18, and then pray something like this:

> Dear Lord,
>
> By faith I want to stand up to the devil by putting on the belt of truth today. Help me to resist the attacks of Satan. Thank You for providing spiritual armor for my protection.
>
> I pray this in the powerful name of Jesus. Amen.

Pray this simple prayer for each piece of armor listed in the passage every day.

Pray

Finally, the most important thing you or I can do in helping to rescue friends or relatives from the darkness is to pray for them. Our first strategic step should be on our knees, asking God through His might and power to break the chains of darkness that hold them prisoner.

Remember, our first objective in rescuing spiritual hostages is to lead them to Christ. If our friends or relatives don't have a personal relationship with Jesus, no matter what we might try to do, they will still be a prisoner of the enemy. If you're not sure how to share Christ with someone, look back at the last chapter for some tips. Then once you are sure of the person's relationship with Christ, you can take them through the seven Steps to Freedom in the last chapter to help them deal with any stubborn habits or sin. Whether you are leading someone to Christ or taking them through the steps, make sure you recruit others to pray for you.

We are involved in a battle for truth, not power. We must help our friends and family to accept God's truth in their lives and stop believing the lies that Satan has fed their minds. Satan's *only* power is in his deceptive lies. The light of God's truth shatters the lies of the devil and sets us free to be the people God designed us to be.

There's no greater privilege than to be used by God to rescue others from the darkness, making a difference that will count for all eternity. Let's look at some practical ways you can be a candle in your world.

Be a Candle in Your World

Do you want to make your life really count? Are you

tired of being bored and looking for some meaning in your life? Then ask God to use you as a candle in the darkness of your home, neighborhood, campus, and in your world. No matter how old you are or what weaknesses you may have, don't let anyone put you down or make you feel incapable of being used by God. Instead, remember what the Bible says in 1 Timothy 4:12: "Don't let anyone look down on you because you are young, but set an example for the believers in speech, in life, in love, in faith and in purity."

I owe my life to someone just like you, and that's why I'm so committed to helping students be all that God designed them to be. Robbie was taking drum lessons from me while I was in the music industry. Each week during his lesson he would tell me about his best friend. He said he shared everything with this friend, but he never told me his best friend's name. I actually started to become jealous of Robbie and his best friend's relationship because I didn't have a friend like him. One day I finally asked Robbie what his best friend's name was, and his response just about knocked me over! "Jesus," Rob said. "And He can be your best friend also." It wasn't long after that that I met Robbie's aunt and uncle who were also Christians, and they led me to Christ.

As a result of one student's courage to tell me that I needed Jesus, people across the United States and in 18 foreign countries have heard the message of God's love through our ministry.

Jim came to me out of concern for a friend on his campus who was deeply involved in playing Dungeons and Dragons and messing around with spells and sorcery. "Steve, I know what my friend is doing is dangerous spiritually, but I don't quite know how to explain it to him," he said. I was able to give Jim some tapes and literature that enabled him to point out the dangers to his friend about dabbling with the darkness. Now his friend is involved with more positive things to challenge his creative mind.

Lori and a couple of her friends became very concerned when they learned that almost 200 kids on their campus had been referred to professional counseling during the first six weeks of school because of their involvement in the occult. They decided to meet once a week after school to pray for the issues plaguing students on their campus and to discuss the Bible together. Before long there were 40 to 50 students and a Christian teacher meeting together once a week to pray and study the Bible. The problem of students involved with the occult hasn't disappeared, but it certainly has gotten better. And Lori and her friends are constantly looking for more ways to be candles on their campus.

David plays on the water polo team at his high school. One day at practice, a couple of his teammates got into a fight, and the coach pulled them out to the sidelines. David remembered what his youth pastor had been discussing at the last youth group meeting: "As iron sharpens iron, so one man sharpens another" (Proverbs 27:17). He shared that verse with his teammates and told them how much more effective they would be if they worked together instead of fighting each other. Since that time, David has had several opportunities to share practical principles from the Bible with other people on his campus.

God used these students. He wants to use you, too. As you become aware of different issues troubling those around you, ask God how He wants to use you to be that candle of light in a dark world. Jesus said in Matthew 5:14-16, "You are like light for the whole world. A city built on top of a hill cannot be hidden, and no one would light a lamp and put it under a clay pot. A lamp is placed on a lamp stand, where it can give light to everyone in the house. Make your light shine, so that others will see the good that you do and will praise your Father in heaven" (CEV). One person really can make a difference when serving the Lord!

One Person Can Make a Difference

In Romania in December of 1989, Communist authorities sent police to arrest Laszlo Tokes, the pastor of the Hungarian Reformed Church in the town of Timisoara. But when they arrived, the police found a solid wall of people blocking the entrance to the church. Members of many different churches had joined together in protest. The people didn't budge for the police. They held their ground the entire day and into the night. Shortly after midnight, a 19-year-old student named Daniel Gavra pulled out a packet of candles. Lighting one, he passed it to the person next to him.

Then he lit another candle and another one after that. One by one the brightly shining candles were passed out among the crowd. Very soon the darkness of that cold December night was pierced by the light of hundreds of candles. Christians came together in unity, disregarding denominational differences and joining hands in the pastor's defense. Even though the crowd stayed through the night and the next day, the police finally broke through and arrested the pastor and his family.

But that was not the end. The religious protest led to political protest in the city as people moved to the town square to begin a full-scale demonstration against the Communist government. Once again Daniel passed out candles. Ultimately troops were brought to squelch the demonstration. Hundreds were shot and Daniel's leg was blown off. But despite the opposition, their example inspired the whole nation of Romania and ultimately caused the collapse of the evil dictator Ceausescu. [1]

One young man lit the candle that eventually lit up a whole country! It only takes a small flame in a dark world to make a difference. Will you be the first candle in the dark in your home, on your campus, in your community?

Final Thoughts

We've covered a lot of important things together in this book. Now you know what you're up against in the spiritual battle. And even though we have an enemy who is bent on our destruction, we *can* have victory in the spiritual conflict in which we are engaged.

The devil will try any avenue possible to influence our thinking. The spiritual battle will ultimately be won or lost in the mind. That is why it is so important to stay alert mentally to the temptations that may come our way through music, fantasy role-playing games, witchcraft, New Age philosophies, and a number of other things. As the battle rages for your mind, take control and make sure you are adequately prepared for battle.

Spend quality time getting to know your defender, Jesus, and make sure you have come to grips with your true identity in Him. The best way to do this is through consistent personal Bible study and prayer. And check and recheck your armor and make sure each piece is securely in place through prayer on a daily basis.

The best way to sum up what I've been trying to say in the last 14 chapters is this simple truth: The devil is here to take whatever he can from us. Jesus has come to give us life to the fullest!

In the heat of the spiritual battle, we need to remember who we are—victors in Jesus who conquered sin once and for all on the cross. So stand up to the devil, let the Lord use you as a candle in your world, and you'll never regret it!

Something to Think About

1. What are the three most meaningful things you learned in this book? How do they apply to your life?

2. Think of at least one person you know who needs to be rescued from the darkness. Take a few minutes to pray for that person, asking God how He wants to use you. Then think about what might be the best strategy you can use to reach him or her.

3. List at least three ways/places where God is calling you to be a candle in the darkness right now. What do you need to do? When? With whom? Where?

4. What does it mean to stay close to Jesus? How can you practically accomplish this in your daily life?

5. What is going to be the most difficult area in your life to stand up to the devil? Spend a few minutes in prayer, asking God to help you in this area. Then ask a trusted friend to pray for you and keep you accountable in this area.

APPENDIXES
& NOTES

Satanic/Occultic Symbols
Nine Statements of Satanic Doctrine
Glossary of Satanic/Occultic Terms
Glossary of New Age Terms
Halloween
Notes
For More Information

Satanic/Occultic
Symbols

 Anarchy. Represents the abolition of all law and the denial of authority. Initially, those into punk music used this symbol. Now it is widely used by the followers of heavy metal music and self-styled Satanists.

 Ankh. An ancient Egyptian symbol of life often associated with fertility. The top portion represents the female, and the lower portion symbolizes the male.

 Anti-justice. The Roman symbol for justice was an upright double-bladed ax. The representation of anti-justice inverts the double-bladed ax.

 Black mass indicators. These signs can be used as a source of direction as well as a sign of involvement in black masses.

 Blood ritual. Represents human and animal sacrifices.

 Cross of confusion. An ancient Roman symbol questioning the existence or validity of Christianity.

Cross of Nero. Represented peace in the '60s. Among today's heavy metal and occult groups it signifies the defeat of Christianity (an inverted cross with the cross anchor broken downward).

 Diana and Lucifer. The moon goddess Diana and the morning star Lucifer are found in nearly all types of witchcraft and Satanism. When the moon faces the opposite direction, it is primarily a satanic symbol.

 Hexagram. Also referred to as the seal of Solomon, the hexagram is said to be one of the most powerful symbols in the occult.

 Horned hand. A sign of recognition among those in the occult. It is also used by those attending heavy metal concerts to affirm allegiance to the music's message of negativism.

 Mark of the beast. Four different representations of the mark of the beast or Satan. Note the letter *F* is the sixth letter in the alphabet.

 Pentagram. A five-pointed star, with or without the circle, is an important symbol in most forms of magic. Generally, the top point represents the spirit and the other points represent wind, fire, earth, and water.

 **Sample altar.** The altar may be any flat object where the implements of the ritual are placed. Usually the altar will be placed within a nine-foot circle. It could be as large as 48 inches long, 22 inches wide, and two inches high. The pentagram in the center is etched into the slab. Human or animal blood is then poured into the etching. Other symbols may be carved according to individual group traditions. Implements on the altar

altar may include: chalice, candles, parchment, cauldron, and Book of Shadows. A smaller version of the altar can be found in the bedrooms, closets, etc. of young, self-styled Satanists or dabblers.

 Swastika (broken cross). A symbol of ancient origin, it originally represented the four winds, the four seasons, and the four points of the compass. At that time its arms were at 90-degree angles turned the opposite direction from what is depicted here. The swastika shown here represents the elements or forces turning against nature and out of harmony. Neo-Nazis and occult groups use it in this manner.

 Talisman or amulet. An object with the name or image of a god drawn or inscribed in it.

 Triangle. May vary in size, but it is generally inscribed or drawn on the ground as the place where a demon would appear in a conjuration ritual.

 Upside-down pentagram. Sometimes called a *baphomet*, it is strictly satanic and represents a goat's head.

Nine Statements of Satanic Doctrine

The statements below represent the basis for modern Satanism. These statements are found in the *Satanic Bible*, written by Church of Satan founder Anton LaVey and published in 1969.

1. Satan represents indulgence instead of abstinence.

2. Satan represents vital existence instead of spiritual pipe dreams.

3. Satan represents undefiled wisdom instead of hypocritical self-deceit.

4. Satan represents kindness to those who deserve it instead of love wasted on ingrates.

5. Satan represents vengeance instead of turning the other cheek.

6. Satan represents responsibility to the responsible instead of concern for psychic vampires.

7. Satan represents man as just another animal, sometimes better, more often worse, than those that walk on all fours, who, because of his "divine spiritual and intellectual development," has become the most vicious animal of all.

8. Satan represents all of the so-called sins as they all lead to physical, mental, or emotional gratification.

9. Satan has been the best friend the church has ever had as he has kept it in business all these years.

Glossary of
Satanic/Occultic Terms

Black mass. Held in honor of the devil on the witches' Sabbath. The ritual reverses the Roman Catholic mass, desecrating the objects used in worship. Sometimes the participants drink the blood of an animal during the ceremony. Often a nude woman is stretched out on the altar, and the high priest concludes the ritual by having sex with her.

Book of Shadows. Also called a *Grimoire*, this journal is kept either by individual witches or Satanists or by a coven to record the activities of the group and the incantations used.

Chalice. A silver goblet used for blood communions.

Coven. A group of Satanists who gather to perform rites. There are traditionally 13 members, but with self-styled groups the number varies. A coven is also called a *clan*.

Curse. Invocation of an oath associated with black magic or sorcery intended to harm or destroy property or opponents.

Druids. A branch of dangerous and powerful Celtic priests from pre-Christian Britain and Gaul who are still active today. They worship the sun and believe in the immortality of the soul and reincarnation. They are also skilled in medicine and astronomy.

Magick. Magic that employs ritual symbols and ceremony, including ceremonial costumes, dramatic invocations to gods, potent incense, and mystic sacraments.

Magic Circle. A circle inscribed on the floor of a temple for ceremonial purposes. Often nine feet in diameter, it is believed to hold magical powers within and protect those involved in the ceremony from evil.

Magister. The male leader of a coven.

Magus. A male witch.

Necromancy. A practice in which the spirits of the dead are summoned to provide omens for discovering secrets of past or future events.

Necrophilia. An act of sexual intercourse with a corpse.

Occult. From the Latin *occultus*, meaning "secret" or "hidden." The occult refers to secret or hidden knowledge available to initiates, to the supernatural, and sometimes to paranormal phenomena and parapsychology.

Ritual. A prescribed form of religious or magical ceremony.

Runes. A northern European alphabet used by occult groups in secret writing. There are several forms of runering.

Santeria. A mingling of African tribal religions and Catholicism, established by African slaves brought to the Americas and the Caribbean.

So mote it be. Words spoken at the end of an occult ceremony. Similar to "amen" in traditional religious services.

Spiritism. Seeking guidance from dead persons contacted through mediums.

Talisman. A power object, usually an amulet or trinket.

Voodoo. An ancient religion combining ancestor worship, sorcery, charms, and spells. Those involved are extremely superstitious and use strange objects to worship.

Warlock. Often used for a male witch, but it actually designates a traitor.

Wicca. The pagan end of the witchcraft spectrum.

Witch. A male or female practitioner of any sort of witchcraft.

Witchcraft. Known as the "Old Religion," it is an ancient practice dating back to biblical times. It is defined as the performance of magic forbidden by God for nonbiblical ends. The word *witchcraft* is related to the old English word *wiccan*, the practice of magical arts, occultic arts, and nature worship.

Glossary of
New Age Terms

Age of Aquarius. Astrologers believe that evolution goes through cycles directly corresponding to the signs of the zodiac, each lasting approximately 2,000 years. Advocates of the New Age say we are now moving in the cycle associated with Aquarius. The Aquarian Age will supposedly be characterized by a heightened degree of spiritual or cosmic consciousness.

Akashic records. Assumed vast reservoir of knowledge. Some New Agers believe that the events of all human lives have been recorded in the Universal Mind or Memory of Nature in a region of space known as the "ether."

Alchemy. Often associated with medieval folklore, this is a chemical science and speculative philosophy designed to transform base metals into gold. It is figuratively used regarding the change of base human nature into the divine.

Altered states. States other than normal waking consciousness, such as daydreaming, sleep-dreaming, hypnotic trance, meditative, mystical, or drug-induced states, or unconscious states.

Ascended master. A highly evolved individual no longer required to undergo lifetimes on the physical plane in order to achieve spiritual growth.

Aura. An apparent envelope or field of colored radiation said to surround the human body and other animate objects with the color or colors indicating different aspects of physical, psychological, and spiritual condition.

Biofeedback. A technique using instruments to self-monitor normally unconscious, involuntary body processes, such as brain waves, heartbeat, and muscle tension. As this information is fed to the individual, he can consciously and voluntarily control internal biological functions.

Channeling. A New Age form of mediumship or spiritism. The channeler yields control of his perceptual and cognitive capacities to a spiritual entity with the intent of receiving paranormal information.

Chakras. The seven energy points on the human body, according to New Agers and yogis. Raising the Kundalini through the chakras is the aim of yoga meditation. Enlightenment (Samadhi) is achieved when the Kundalini reaches the "crown chakra" at the top of the head.

Clairaudience. The ability to hear mentally without using the ears.

Clairvoyance. The ability to see mentally beyond ordinary time and space without using the eyes. Also called "second sight."

Consciousness. Mental awareness of present knowing. New Agers usually refer to consciousness as the awareness of external objects or facts.

Consciousness revolution. A New Age way of looking at and experiencing life. The primary focus of the new consciousness is oneness with God, all mankind, the earth, and the entire universe.

Cosmic consciousness. A spiritual and mystical perception that all the universe is one. To attain cosmic consciousness is to see the universe as God and see God as the universe.

Crystals. New Age advocates believe that crystals contain incredible healing and energizing powers. Crystals are often touted as being able to restore the flow of energy in the human body.

Dharma. Law, truth, or teaching. Used to express the central teachings of the Hindu and Buddhist religions. Dharma implies that essential truth can be stated about the way things are, and that people should comply with that norm.

Divination. Methods of discovering the personal, human significance of present or future events. The means to obtain insights may include dreams, hunches, involuntary body actions, mediumistic possession, consulting the dead, observing the behavior of animals and birds, tossing coins, casting lots, and reading natural phenomena.

Esoteric. Used to describe knowledge that is possessed or understood by a select few.

ESP. Extrasensory perception. The experience of or response to an external event, object, state, or influence without apparent contact through the known senses. ESP may occur without those involved being aware of it.

Gnosticism. The secret doctrines and practices of mysticism whereby a person may come to the enlightenment or realization that he is of the same essence as God or the Absolute. The Greek word *gnosis* means knowledge. At the heart of Gnostic thought is the idea that revelation of the hidden gnosis frees one from the fragmentary and illusory material world and teaches him about the origins of the spiritual world to which the Gnostic belongs by nature.

The Great Invocation. A New Age prayer that has been translated into over 80 languages. The purpose of this prayer is to invoke the presence of the cosmic Christ on earth, thus leading to the oneness and brotherhood of all mankind.

Harmonic convergence. The assembly of New Age meditators at the same propitious astrological time in different locations to usher in peace on earth and a one-world government.

Hologram. A three-dimensional projection resulting from the interaction of laser beams. Scientists have discovered that the image of an entire hologram can be reproduced from any one of its many component parts. New Agers use the hologram to illustrate the oneness of all reality.

Higher self. The most spiritual and knowing part of oneself, said to lie beyond ego, day-to-day personality, and personal consciousness. The higher self can be channeled for wisdom and guidance. Variations include the oversoul, the super-consciousness, the atman, the Christ (or Krishna or Buddha) consciousness, and the God within.

Humanism. The philosophy that upholds the primacy of human beings rather than God or any abstract metaphysical system. Humanism holds that man is the measure of all things.

Human potential movement. A movement with roots in humanistic philosophy that stresses man's essential goodness and unlimited potential.

Initiation. An occult term generally used in reference to the expansion or transformation of a person's consciousness. An initiate is one whose consciousness has been transformed to perceive inner realities. There are varying degrees of initiation, such as first degree, second degree, etc.

Inner self. The inner divine nature possessed by human beings. All people are said to possess an inner self, though they may not be aware of it.

Interdependence/Interconnectedness. Used by New Agers to describe the oneness and essential unity of everything in the universe. All reality is viewed as interdependent and interconnected.

Karma. The debt accumulated against the soul as a result of good or bad actions committed during one's life (or lives). If one accumulates good karma, he supposedly will be reincarnated to a desirable state. If one accumulates bad karma, he will be reincarnated to a less desirable state.

Kirilian. A type of high-voltage photography using a pulsed, high-frequency electrical field and two electrodes between which are placed the object to be photographed and an unexposed film plate. The image captured is purported to be an aura of energy emanating from plants, animals, and humans that changes in accordance with physiological or emotional shifts.

Kundalini. A pyscho-spiritual power thought by yogis to lie dormant at the base of the spine. The Kundalini is believed to be a "goddess" and is often referred to as "serpent power."

Magic circle. A ring drawn by occultists to protect them from the spirits and demons they call up by incantations and rituals.

Mantra. A holy word, phrase, or verse in Hindu or Buddhist meditation techniques. A mantra is usually provided to an initiate by a guru who supposedly holds specific insights regarding the needs of his pupils. The vibrations of the mantra are said to lead the meditator into union with the divine source within.

Monism. Literally means *one*. In a spiritual framework it refers to the classical occult philosophy that all is one; all reality may be reduced to a single unifying principle partaking of the same essence and reality. Monism also relates to the belief that there is no ultimate distinction between the creator and the creation (pantheism).

Mysticism. The belief that God is totally different from anything the human mind can think and must be approached by a mind without content. Spiritual union or direct communion with ultimate reality can be obtained through subjective experience such as intuition or a unifying vision.

New Age movement. The most common name for the growing penetration of Eastern and occultic mysticism into Western culture. The words *New Age* refer to the Aquarian Age which occultists believe is dawning, bringing with it an era of enlightenment and peace. Encompassed within the New Age movement are various cults which emphasize mystic experiences.

Nirvana. Literally a blowing out or cooling of the fires of existence. It is the main term in Buddhism for the final release from the cycle of birth and death into bliss.

Numerology. The analysis of hidden prophetic meanings of numbers.

Pantheism. The belief that God and the world are ultimately identical; all is God. Everything that exists constitutes a unity, and this all-inclusive unity is divine. God is equated with the forces and laws of the universe but is not a personal being.

Paradigm shift. Refers to a shift in worldviews. The so-called new paradigm (new model or form) is pantheistic (all is God) and monistic (all is one).

Planetization. New Age advocates believe that the various threats facing the human race require a global solution called "planetization." It refers to the unifying of the world into a corporate brotherhood.

Poltergeist. German word for a noisy, mischievous, destructive spirit (demon).

PSI. The twenty-third letter of the Greek alphabet. A general New Age term for ESP, psychokinesis, telepathy, clairvoyance, clairaudience, precognition, and other paranormal phenomena that are nonphysical in nature.

Psychic. A medium, "sensitive," or channeler. Also refers to paranormal events that can't be explained by established physical principles.

Psychic birth. A quickening of spiritual or cosmic consciousness and power. This new consciousness recognizes oneness with God and the universe. Psychic birth is an occult counterpart to the Christian new birth.

Psychokinesis (PK). The power of the mind to influence matter or move objects (see also *telekinesis*).

Reincarnation. The belief that the soul moves from one bodily existence to another until, usually after many lives, it is released from historical existence and absorbed into the Absolute.

Right brain learning. The right hemisphere of the brain is believed to be the center of intuitive and creative thought (as opposed to the rational nature of the left hemisphere). New Agers have seized on this as a justification to bring right brain learning techniques into the classroom. These techniques include meditation, yoga, and guided imagery.

Seance. A gathering of people seeking communication with deceased loved ones or famous historical figures through a medium.

Self-realization. A synonym for *God-realization*. It refers to a personal recognition of one's divinity.

Shaman. A medicine man or witch doctor.

Spirit guide. A spiritual entity who provides information or guidance often through a medium or channeler. The spirit provides guidance only after the channeler relinquishes his perceptual and cognitive capacities into its control.

Syncretism. The fusion of different forms of belief or practice; the claim that all religions are one and share the same core teachings.

Synergy. The quality of "whole making"; the New Age belief in the cooperation of natural systems to put things together in ever more meaningful patterns.

Third eye. An imaginary eye in the forehead believed to be the center of psychic vision.

Tantra. A series of Hindu or Buddhist scriptures concerned with special yogic practices for swift attainment of enlightenment; also the practices, techniques, and traditions of these teachings.

Telekinesis. A form of psychokinesis (PK); the apparent movement of stationary objects without the use of known physical force.

Trance. An altered state of consciousness, induced or spontaneous, that gives access to many ordinarily inhibited capacities of the mind-body system. Trance states are generally self-induced.

Visualization. Also known as "guided imagery"; refers to mind over matter. Visualization is the attempt to bring about change in the material realm by the power of the mind.

Yoga. Literally, yoking or joining; any system or spiritual discipline by which the practitioner or yogi seeks to condition the self at all levels—physical, psychical, and spiritual. The goal is a state of well-being, the loss of self-identity, and absorption into the Absolute or Ultimate Being.

Yogi. A master of one or more methods of yoga who teaches it to others.

Zen. A type of Buddhist thought best known for its emphasis on breaking down the commitment and attachment to the logical and rational ordering of experience.

Zodiac. The imaginary belt in the heavens that encompasses the apparent paths of the principal planets except Pluto. Divided into 12 constellations or signs based on the assumed dates that the sun enters each of these "houses" or symbols, the zodiac is used for predictions in astrology.

Halloween

All Hallows Eve or Halloween, October 31, is the day witches celebrate above all other days. Many believe that Satan and his witches have their greatest power on this night.

The origin of Halloween goes back thousands of years to a practice of the ancient Druids in France, Germany, Britain, and the other Celtic countries. The celebration honored the lord of the dead, their god Samhain. The Druids believed that on this night of celebrating death, the spirits of the dead returned to their former home to visit the living. If the living did not provide food for these evil spirits, all types of terrible things could happen. The evil spirits would "trick" the living if they did not get a "treat."

Before Christianity was introduced to these lands, this celebration of death was not called Halloween. The word *Halloween* is a form of the phrase "All Hallows Eve," a holy evening started by the church to honor all the saints of church history.

Some church historians say it is possible that All Saints Eve was designated October 30 to counteract the celebration of death and its pagan influences.

Today Halloween is a secular holiday that provides an excuse to wear a costume and have a party. But followers of witchcraft and true witches still preserve the ancient pagan beliefs and consider Halloween a sacred, deadly, and powerful time.

Notes

Chapter 2—The Fascination with Evil

1. *ABC News 20/20*, December 4, 1992.
2. Ibid.

Chapter 3—Do You Know Your Enemy?

1. George Barna, *The Barna Report* (Ventura, CA: Regal Books, 1991), pp. 204-05.

Chapter 4—The Battle for Your Mind

1. Carl M. Cannon, "Honey, I Warped the Kids," *Mother Jones* (July/August 1993), p. 19.
2. Ibid., p. 20.
3. Neil T. Anderson and Steve Russo, *The Seduction of Our Children* (Eugene, OR: Harvest House Publishers, 1991), pp. 34-36.
4. *Entertainment Weekly* (August 27, 1993), p. 42.
5. George Barna, *Today's Teens: A Generation in Transition* (Glendale, CA: Barna Research Group, 1991), p. 26.

Chapter 5—Is Rock Music Really Satanic?

1. "Garth Takes a Brave Stand," *Newsweek* (October 12, 1992), p. 86.
2. Ibid.
3. Ibid.
4. *Rising to the Challenge* video (Parents' Music Resource Center).
5. Jerry Minor, *Metallica*, Vol. 2 (Metal Thunder Comics, July 1992).

Chapter 6—A Game Turns Deadly

1. Rob Walters, *The Bakersfield Californian* (Tuesday, November 24, 1992), pp. A1-2.

2. Neil T. Anderson and Steve Russo, *The Seduction of Our Children* (Eugene, OR: Harvest House Publishers, 1991), p. 78.

Chapter 7—Witchcraft Isn't Cool

1. "Witchcraft Is a Religion," *Sassy* (March 1992), pp. 64-65, 80-81.
2. Ibid.
3. Ibid.
4. *The Daily Bulletin* (Friday, August 20, 1993), p. G6.
5. *The Hot 200* (New Song Publishing, 1987), p. 7.

Chapter 8—The New Age

1. *Time* (December 7, 1987), p. 62.
2. Russell Chandler, *Understanding the New Age* (Waco, TX: Word Publishing, 1988), pp. 20-21.
3. James Patterson and Peter Kim, *The Day America Told the Truth* (New York: Prentice Hall Press, 1991), p. 204.

Chapter 13—Choose Your Weapons

1. George Barna, *Today's Teens: A Generation in Transition* (Glendale, CA: Barna Research Group, 1991), p. 43.

Chapter 14—Freedom from the Power of Darkness

1. Adapted from Neil T. Anderson and Steve Russo, *The Seduction of Our Children* (Eugene, OR: Harvest House Publishers, 1991), pp. 211-30. Used by permission.
2. George Barna, *The Barna Report*, "What Americans Believe" (Ventura, CA: Regal Books, 1991), p. 85.

Chapter 15—Candle in the Dark

1. Chuck Colson, *The Body* (Dallas, TX: Word Publishing, 1992), pp. 58-61.

For more information on Steve's ministry, including spiritual warfare seminars for parents and students, "Real Answers" citywide evangelistic campaigns, "Multiple Choice" public school assemblies, and audio- and videotape resources that are available, please contact:

Steve Russo Evangelistic Team
P.O. Box 1549
Ontario, CA 91762
(909) 466-7060
FAX (909) 466-7056